YOUNG VIC
THEATRE COMPANY

The Young Vic Theatre Company presents

Arabian Nights

adapted and directed by
DOMINIC COOKE

The Young Vic is supported by

SUPPORTED BY
THE NATIONAL LOTTERY
THROUGH
THE **ARTS COUNCIL**
OF ENGLAND

THE YOUNG VIC THEATRE

The Young Vic Theatre combines the creation and presentation of award-winning performance, in superb auditoria, with far-reaching teaching, participation and access policies.

In almost 30 years of existence the Young Vic has created an enormous range and style of work and today, under Artistic Director Tim Supple, we continue our commitment to creating adventurous theatre for as wide an audience as possible and, in particular, the young. The intimacy and adaptability of our two theatre spaces offers unique opportunities for ensemble performance and the imaginative use of space, light and sound. Today the Young Vic's work is by no means restricted to London audiences; the company tours extensively abroad, most recently to Hong Kong, Japan, New Zealand and Australia. This Christmas, we will present our acclaimed collection of *Grimm Tales* in a New York season at the New Victory Theatre, 42nd Street, before moving on to the Sydney Festival in the New Year.

How the Young Vic started

Planning for the Young Vic began at the National Theatre in 1968. At that time the National Theatre's current South Bank home had yet to be built and they were based at the Old Vic. Frank Dunlop and Laurence Olivier talked of a theatre which would form a centre of work particularly accessible to students and young people. The theatre's programme was to include the classics, new plays and educational work, and would provide an opportunity for young performers, writers and directors to develop their craft. This concept is widely accepted today but was radical and new in 1968.

The Young Vic was established two years later in September 1970 by Frank Dunlop, who directed the first performance *Scapino*, based on Molière's *Les Fourberies de Scapin*. The Young Vic became the first major theatre producing work for younger audiences. In 1974 we became fully independent of the National Theatre and continued to build a national and international reputation for our work, developing a wide-ranging audience of all ages and backgrounds.

The Young Vic Theatre Company has evolved an artistic policy which integrates all areas of our work including performance, teaching, participation, audience development and access. In September 1997 we received one of the highest grants in the country through the National Lottery's Arts for Everyone Award Scheme, issued through the Arts Council of England. This award enabled the Young Vic to establish the first of three resident companies of performers and to implement a daring three year project of new creative work and associated audience development. The scheme will allow the Young Vic to build upon recent growth and further establish our position as one of the premier theatre companies in Britain.

An indication of our success is that in its first year, during the first

Resident Company season, over 8000 people visited the Young Vic for the first time to see **More Grimm Tales, Twelfth Night** or **As I Lay Dying**. Our work is certain to evolve and will provide many more opportunities to enjoy and participate in the world of theatre.

Plans for the Main House in 1999 include an RSC Season (**Bartholemew Fair**, directed by Laurence Boswell, and **Talk of the City**, written and directed by Stephen Poliakoff), and a co-production, with Plymouth Theatre Royal, of **Hamlet**, directed by Laurence Boswell. The Young Vic Studio will continue its commitment to housing and nurturing experiments in writing, music, performance and design.

THE YOUNG VIC FUNDED TICKET SCHEME

The Young Vic Theatre Company created the Funded Ticket Scheme (main sponsor Allied Domecq plc) in 1994, to enable groups of people, of all ages, to visit the theatre for the first time. Now, due to our successful application to the National Lottery's Arts for Everyone programme, the Young Vic has been able to radically expand the scheme and provide an introduction to the theatre for thousands of people who otherwise may not have attended, because of either financial or social restraints. This Christmas, close to 3000 people will visit the Young Vic to see *Arabian Nights* through the Funded Ticket Scheme.

If you would like further information regarding this scheme for a group within London and the home counties, please write to: Barry Wilson, Audience Development Officer, Young Vic Theatre, The Cut, London SE1 8LZ.

The Arts for Everyone programme is designed to highlight the integral role that a theatre plays in the community. To realise the enormous potential that this award promises, the Young Vic must find companies, charitable foundations and individuals who share in our belief in this vital investment in the community. Over the next three years the Young Vic must raise a total of £100,000 in partnership funding to release this remarkable lottery award. We take this opportunity to acknowledge the support of **Allied Domecq plc** in providing a much-needed lead gift of £36,000 over three years together with the generous support of **David and Maria Willetts**, **The Royal Victoria Hall Foundation**, **J Sainsbury plc** and **Direct Connection**.

If you would like more information on how you can help us to achieve this important goal, please contact the Young Vic Development Office on **0171 633 0133**.

SUPPORTED BY
THE NATIONAL LOTTERY
THROUGH
THE ARTS COUNCIL
OF ENGLAND

The Young Vic takes this opportunity to thank its many supporters, which include:

Be a Part of the Future of British Theatre – Support the Young Vic

To maintain our position as a leading centre for theatre which embraces people of all ages and backgrounds, to achieve our Arts for Everyone partnership funding challenge and to develop our teaching, participation and research programmes to encompass more inner city communities – we need your support.

As you enjoy today's performance, the Young Vic asks you to consider supporting our work by:

* Becoming a **Friend of the Young Vic**
* Making a tax efficient gift by covenant or Gift Aid
* Making a bequest in favour of the Young Vic in your will.

For further information on how you can help support the future of British theatre please take a leaflet from the foyer or call **0171 633 0133** to receive further information.

THE YOUNG VIC ARABIAN NIGHTS CHILDREN'S GALA

28 NOVEMBER 1998 2.00PM in support of the Young Vic's Funded Ticket Scheme, which enables close to 3,000 inner city children to experience theatre for the very first time.

The Young Vic takes this opportunity to express its sincere thanks to the following for helping to make this event such a success:

Juliet Stevenson, Honorary Chair, *Arabian Nights* Gala Committee

Gala Committee Members: Maria Church, Régis Gautier-Cochefert, Gabbi Delall, Vanessa Devereux, Alison Moore-Gwyn, Corinne Hall, Julia Havis, Lizzie Long, Margaret McKenna, Mandy Martinez, Catherine Pawson, Joanne Pearce, Thomas Ponsonby, Katherine Priestley, Maria Willetts, Victoria Wynn, Sybella Zisman.

TimeOut KidsOut Magazine

Allied Domecq plc for providing complimentary champagne

Beechdean Dairies Ltd for providing complimentary Duke of Wellington Dairy Ice Creams

Marks and Spencer plc for providing food and refreshments for Shahrazad's Children's Tea.

The Young Vic also takes this opportunity to offer special thanks to the very many generous companies and individuals who provided prizes for the *Arabian Nights* Gala prize draw.

THE YOUNG VIC COMPANY

Please switch off mobile phones and bleeping watches.

WORK WITH CHILDREN, YOUNG PEOPLE, STUDENTS, SCHOOLS, COLLEGES AND YOUNG PROFESSIONALS.

TEACHING, PARTICIPATION AND RESEARCH

Teaching others about theatre, and learning ourselves from this activity, are integral to the Young Vic. We provide young people from 3 to 20 years old with the practical means to explore theatre through the skills and experience of our award-winning core creative team. This process of research directly informs our work on stage.

Our programme includes:
- Regular theatre making activities
- Rehearsal, music, text, voice and body teaching projects
- On stage production workshops
- A Schools' Theatre Festival
- Written resource material
- Workshops both with studio practitioners and for young professionals
- An extensive work experience and apprenticeship programme

All the work is free of charge to participants and runs in tandem with the Funded Ticket Scheme which offers access to performances through free or highly subsidised tickets.

Our activities primarily focus on the inner-city boroughs of Lambeth and Southwark with the expectation of developing links with other South East London Boroughs.

If you would like to know more about the Young Vic's teaching activities, please telephone **0171 633 0133**.

 Coming soon at the Young Vic

new RSC season at the Young Vic

RSC

ROYAL
SHAKESPEARE
COMPANY

Sponsored by
**ALLIED
DOMECQ**

SARA MARKLAND AND DAVID WESTHEAD IN 'TALK OF THE CITY'

Previews from 3 February

Talk of the City

STEPHEN POLIAKOFF

This production is sponsored by JBA

Previews from 18 February

Bartholomew Fair

BEN JONSON

This production is sponsored by The Firkin Brewery

TICKETS ON SALE FROM 30 NOVEMBER THROUGH THE YOUNG VIC BOX OFFICE

YOUNG VIC

BOX OFFICE 0171 928 6363

A THEATRE ROYAL PLYMOUTH / YOUNG VIC
PRODUCTION

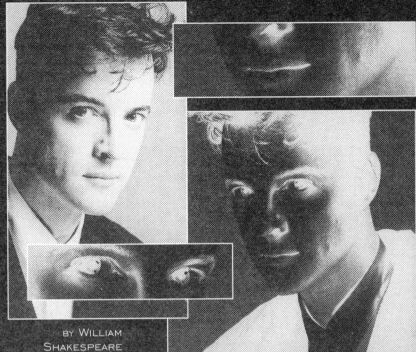

BY WILLIAM
SHAKESPEARE

DIRECTED BY
LAURENCE BOSWELL

STARRING PAUL RHYS

hamlet

The stark horror of a young man faced with the murder of his father, the betrayal of his lover and the machinations of the state is played out in Laurence Boswell's taut new production with Paul Rhys in the title role. The director of the acclaimed **Long Day's Journey Into Night** and the award-winning West End hit **Popcorn** returns to the Theatre Royal and the Young Vic to stage a fresh and original version of Shakespeare's greatest play. Laurence and Paul last worked together on **Long Day's Journey Into Night** where Paul created the unforgettable character of Edmund in O'Neill's classic play.

18 - 27 MARCH 1999   1 APRIL - 8 MAY 1999

YOUNG VIC

BOOKING OPENS NOV 1998

BOX OFFICE: 01752 267222   BOX OFFICE: 0171 928 6363

THE YOUNG VIC STUDIO

Take nothing for granted - anything is possible
- nothing is sacrosanct

The Young Vic Studio presents a dynamic and diverse range of companies who are creating work for contemporary audiences driven by the experiences of our age.

25 November - 5 December 1998
A Young Vic Studio commission
louder than words presents

IN CLOSE RELATION

A place of fun and fear, of mothers and sons, of chocolate rivers and acid tears. The moment between being a child and an adult, between desire and death. A world of happy songs where playtime just goes on and on.

Created out of memories, texts and downright lies, **In Close Relation** uses enactment, improvisations, exact instructions and dodgy dances to explore the potentially explosive relationship between six boys, four women and one man.

Wednesday to Saturday at 7.15pm
Matinees Saturday 28 November and 5 December at 2.15pm
Tickets £8 (£5 concessions)
Saturday matinee Family tickets:
Full Price - £11 to include one adult and one child with £4 for each additional child and £8 for each additional adult.
Concession - £8 to include one adult and one child with £4 for each additional child and £5 for each additional adult.

---

8 - 23 December 1998
Strathcona Theatre Company presents

id

Strathcona Theatre Company's sixteenth production is set in a time when ignorance and prejudice conspired to create the gaudy cruelty of the circus sideshow. **id** is about beauty and the tyranny the image of beauty holds over the destiny of two babies. A piece of physical theatre devised from original ideas by Strathcona's core company of eight learning disabled actors, **id** highlights Strathcona's extraordinary ability for ensemble playing and inspired, original story-telling.

Evenings at 7.30pm
Matinees on 9,11,14,16,18 Dec at 1.15pm
Tickets: £8 (£4 concessions - Combined workshop tickets £6)

---

11 - 23 January 1999
Alice Purcell & Alice Power present

A SPECIAL OFFER

as part of the London International Mime Festival

A new devised show, inspired by visits to Sharps Bedrooms and the short stories of Raymond Carver. Set in a display bedroom a model couple go through the motions of a relationship. The audience eavesdrop like perverse window shoppers, watching the couple's hilarious and upsetting struggle to find out what it is they really want. And why is the Sales Assistant singing opera?

Evenings at 7.30pm
Tickets: £8 (£6 concessions)

26 January - 6 February 1999
desperate optimists presents

PLAY-BOY

Against a background of Latin dance rhythms, **Play-boy** will explore our fear of loneliness, the seductive pull of violence and the act of story-telling as a strategy for survival. As interested in anecdote and gossip as it is in the deep philosophical ramblings of the self-obsessed, **Play-boy** allows for a range of questions to be asked about the nature of the lives we have constructed for ourselves.

Evenings at 7.45pm
Tickets: £8 (£6 concessions)

For tickets and information on all Young Vic Studio performances, call the box-office on **0171 928 6363**

Arabian Nights

PERFORMERS IN ALPHABETICAL ORDER:

Peter Bailie   Ishia Bennison
Paul Chahidi   Kate Fleetwood
Harmage Singh Kalirai   Tim McMullan
Sophie Okonedo   Chu Omambala
Yasmin Wilde

Musicians
Martin Allen   Keith Thompson

Adapted and directed by	**Dominic Cooke**
Designed by	**Georgia Sion**
Music composed by	**Gary Yershon**
Lighting designed by	**Paul Anderson**
Sound designed by	**Fergus O'Hare** for Aura Sound Ltd.
Choreography by	**Liz Ranken**
Assistant Director	**Lynne Gagliano**
Puppetry Consultant and Puppets by	**Anna Ingleby**
Illusions by	**Paul Kieve**
Script Editor	**Noelle Morris**
Company Stage Manager	**Sid Charlton**
Deputy Stage Manager	**Jack Morrison**
Assistant Stage Manager	**Bryan Paterson**
Props Supervisor	**Lily Mollgaard**
Wardrobe Supervisor	**Charlotte Stewart**
Wardrobe Manager	**Judith Adams**
Assistant Costume Supervisor	**Fiona McCann**
Dresser	**Heidi Bryan**

PRODUCTION CREATED BY STAFF OF THE YOUNG VIC COMPANY

Production Acknowledgements
Set by Young Vic Workshop.

Props made by Paul Williams, Paul Gallagher and Anna Goller (work placement from Ohio University). Cloaks made by Helen Charlton. Costumes made by Judith Adams, Claire Boyle, Claire-Louise Hardie and Maria Rainsdern. Hats made by Mark Wheeler. With special thanks to Mandy Burnett and Patrick Anwyl for small props. Slate supplied by Terra Firma Tiles. Lighting equipment supplied by Sparks Theatrical Hire, White Light Electrics Ltd. and Lighting Technology.

With thanks to:
Ruth Paton and Rebecca Chippendale, (design assistants)
Craig Higginson, for programme material.
International Shakespeare Globe Centre
Hampstead Theatre
The Islamic Cultural Centre
Persil, Comfort and Stergene, courtesy of Lever Brothers, for Wardrobe Care.

First performed at the Young Vic Theatre on **16 November 1998**

STORIES AND CHARACTERS

THE STORY OF SHAHRAYAR AND SHAHRAZAD

Shahrazad ......Sophie Okonedo
Dinarzad ....Kate Fleetwood
Vizier ....Tim McMullan
Shahrayar ....Chu Omambala

THE STORY OF ALI BABA AND THE FORTY THIEVES

Ali Baba ....Peter Bailie
Kasim/Ali Baba's Son .Paul Chahidi
Ali Baba's Wife .....Yasmin Wilde
Kasim's Wife ......Kate Fleetwood
Captain Of The Forty Thieves
................Tim McMullan
Marjana ....Ishia Bennison
Baba Mustapha
.........Harmage Singh Kalirai

THE STORY OF THE LITTLE BEGGAR

Tailor ....Paul Chahidi
Tailor's Wife/Hangman
.................Kate Fleetwood
Beggar ....Peter Bailie
Doctor's Maid/Merchant
.................Ishia Bennison
Doctor ....Tim McMullan
Steward ...Harmage Singh Kalirai
Chief Of Police ...Sophie Okonedo

THE ADVENTURE OF ES-SINDIBAD OF THE SEA

Es-Sindibad The Porter
..................Paul Chahidi
Es-Sindibad The Sailor
.................Tim McMullan
Page/ Merchant ....Kate Fleetwood
Merchants ..Harmage Singh Kalirai
.................Peter Bailie

HOW ABU HASSAN BROKE WIND

Abu Hassan
.........Harmage Singh Kalirai
Marriage Broker/Girl ....
.................Yasmin Wilde
Bride.............Kate Fleetwood

THE STORY OF THE WIFE WHO WOULDN'T EAT

Amina ....Ishia Bennison
Sidi Nu'uman 1 ......Paul Chahidi
Sidi Nu'uman 2 ....Peter Bailie
Haroun Al-Rashid ..Tim McMullan
Baker .....Harmage Singh Kalirai
Good Sorceress' Mother
.................Kate Fleetwood
Good Sorceress ...Sophie Okonedo

THE STORY OF THE ENVIOUS SISTERS

Khusrau Shah .....Chu Omambala
Khusrau Shah's Vizier/Wise Old Man
.................Tim McMullan
Eldest Sister/Old Religious Woman
.................Ishia Bennison
Middle Sister/Steward's Wife
.................Yasmin Wilde
Youngest Sister ....Sophie Okonedo
Khusrau Shah's Steward/Cook
.........Harmage Singh Kalirai
Bahman ....Paul Chahidi
Perviz ....Peter Bailie
Parizade ....Kate Fleetwood

Other parts played by members of the company

BIOGRAPHIES

MARTIN ALLEN *Musician*

As Music Director for the Royal National Theatre, work includes *The Winter's Tale*, *Cymbeline*, *The Tempest* (& tours of Greece, Japan & Russia), *The Trackers of Oxyrhynchus*, *Machinal*. Other work includes *The Winter's Tale*, *The Crucible* (RSC), *Richard III* (RNT & tours of USA, Europe & Japan), *Hamlet* (RNT & tours of Japan, Hong Kong & Yugoslavia), *King Lear* (RNT & tours of Japan & Europe), *Othello*, *Pericles*, *Volpone*, *Antony & Cleopatra* (all RNT).

PAUL ANDERSON *Lighting Designer*

Theatre includes *Special Occasions*, *Hospitality*, *A Coupla White Chicks Sitting Around Talking* (for North American Theatre UK), *Double Bass* (Man in the Moon), *The Real World* (Soho Poly), *West Side Story*, *Guys and Dolls*, *Twelfth Night*, *As I Lay Dying* (Young Vic), re-lights of *The Three Lives of Lucie Cabrol* (Theatre de Complicite), re-lights of *The Caucasian Chalk Circle* (RNT/Theatre de Complicite), re-lights of *The Street of Crocodiles* (Theatre de Complicite), *The Chairs* (Theatre de Complicite/Royal Court - Drama Desk, Tony, & Olivier Award nominations).

PETER BAILIE *Performer*

Trained with Teatr Blik, Poland. Theatre includes Mark Ravenhill's *Faust* (Actors Touring Company), *All's Well That Ends Well* (Oxford Stage Company), *Peter Pan* (West Yorkshire Playhouse), *Edward II* (Leicester Haymarket), *The Maids* (Actors Touring Company), *A Midsummer Night's Dream* (Edinburgh Lyceum), *The Mosquito Coast*, *Gormenghast* (both David Glass Ensemble). Television includes *Faith in the Future* (LWT). Teaches at the Drama Studio, Ealing.

ISHIA BENNISON *Performer*

Theatre includes *Samson Agonistes*, *Antony and Cleopatra*, *A Midsummer Night's Dream*, *Romeo and Juliet*, *Merry Wives* (all Northern Broadsides), *Medea* (Sadlers Wells), *Educating Rita*, *One for the Road* (national tours), *Turcaret* (Gate Theatre). Television includes *Eastenders*, *Love Hurts*, *1001 Nights*.

PAUL CHAHIDI *Performer*

Theatre includes *All's Well That Ends Well* (Oxford Stage Company), *Misalliance* (Theatr Clwyd/Birmingham Rep), *The Devil Is an Ass*, *Julius Caesar*, *Woyzeck*, *Faust Parts I & II* (all Royal Shakespeare Company). Television includes *Murder Most Horrid* (Talkback), *Blonde Bombshell* (LWT), *Bliss* (Carlton), *Wise Children* (Channel Four). Film includes *Notting Hill* (Bookshop Productions), *Stella Does Tricks* (BFI).

DOMINIC COOKE *Adapter & Director*

Theatre includes *Hunting Scenes from Lower Bavaria*, *The Weavers* (both Gate Theatre), *Afore Night Come*, *Entertaining Mr Sloane* (both Theatr Clwyd), *The Bullet* (Donmar Warehouse), *My Mother Said I Never Should* (Oxford Stage Company), *Of Mice and Men* (Nottingham Playhouse), *Kiss of the Spiderwoman* (Bolton Octagon), *Autogeddon* (Edinburgh Assembly Rooms - Fringe First), *The Marriage of Figaro* (tour adaptation and direction - winner of the Manchester Evening News Award). Assistant Director at the Royal Shakespeare Company, 1992-1994.

KATE FLEETWOOD *Performer*

Theatre includes *Romeo and Juliet* (Greenwich Theatre), *The Comic Mysteries* (Oxford Stage Company/Greenwich Theatre), *Swaggers* (Old Red Lion), *Twelfth Night*, *Love is a Drug* (both Oxford Stage Company). Television includes *Getting Hurt*, *Lizzie's Pictures* (both BBC), *Seriously Funny*, *Catching Alight* (both Channel Four).

LYNNE GAGLIANO *Assistant Director*

Work as a director includes *Glass* (The White Bear), *Signal Failure* (Medicine Room), *Charlotte* (Duke of Cambridge/tour to the Czech Republic), *Spring Cleaning*, *Snow White* (both Theatre Box Children's Theatre). Work as Assistant Director includes *The Weavers* (Gate Theatre), *My Mother Said I Never Should* (Oxford Stage Company), *A River Sutra* (National Theatre/Indosa Productions). Education Director for Polyglot Theatre Company.

HARMAGE SINGH KALIRAI *Performer*

Theatre includes *Bravely Fought the Queen* (Border Crossing), *My Beautiful Launderette* (Cardiff Sherman), *Dick Whittington* (Wolverhampton Grand), *The Moonstone/Riddley Walker* (Royal Exchange, Manchester). Television includes *The Cops* (BBC2), *Trial and Retribution* (Carlton), *The Knock* (LWT), *A Touch of Frost* (YTV), *Medics* (Granada). Film includes *Guru in Seven* (Balhar), *Brothers in Trouble* (Renegade), *Paper Mask* (Granada).

TIM McMULLAN *Performer*

Theatre includes *Lady Betty* (Cheek by Jowl), *The Three Lives of Lucie Cabrol* (Theatre de Complicite), *The Caucasian Chalk Circle* (Theatre de Complicite/Royal National Theatre), *The Front Page* (Donmar Warehouse), *The Wind in the Willows*, *Richard III* (both Royal National Theatre). Film includes *Onegin*, *Shakespeare in Love*, *Plunkett and Maclean*, *The Fifth Element*, *Shadowlands*. Radio includes *To the Wedding* (Radio 3).

FERGUS O'HARE *Sound Designer*

Theatre includes *Habeas Corpus*, *The Bullet*, *How I Learned To Drive* (all Donmar Warehouse), *Electra* (Donmar Warehouse/New York), *Backpay*, *One More Wasted Year* (both English Stage Company, Royal Court Theatre), *Wasp* (Edinburgh Festival 1997), *Miss Julie* (Young Vic), *An Enemy of the People* (Royal National Theatre/L.A.), *Starstruck* (The Tricycle), *Dancing at Lughnasa* (NYT), *Yard* (The Bush).

SOPHIE OKONEDO *Performer*

Theatre includes *Been So Long* (Royal Court), *900 Oneonta* (Old Vic), *A Jovial Crew*, *The Odyssey* (both RSC). Television includes *Deep Secrets* (BBC Screen 1), *Maria's Child* (BBC Screen 2), *Staying Alive I & II* (LWT). Films include *Mad Cow*, *Go Now*, *Ace Ventura II*, *The Jackal*, *This Year's Love*.

CHU OMAMBALA *Performer*

Theatre includes *Macbeth* (Bristol Old Vic). Television includes *Doomwatch* (Channel 5). Film includes *The Seventh Scroll* (Eurolux Productions).

LIZ RANKEN *Choreographer*

Work as Movement Director includes *Anna Karenina* (Time Out Award), *The Mill on the Floss*, *Jane Eyre*, *War and Peace*, *The Tempest* (all Shared Experience), *The Changeling*, *Troilus and Cressida* (both RSC), *My Mother Said I Never Should* (Oxford Stage Company). Work as Director includes *Funk Off Green* (won Capital Award, Edinburgh), *Summer Ado* (won Place Portfolio Award), *Ooh* (Third Eye Centre). As a performer, Liz has worked with **DV8**.

GEORGIA SION *Designer*

Theatre includes *Crave* (Paines Plough), *Perfect Days* (Traverse Theatre, Edinburgh), *Sleeping Around* (Paines Plough), *Afore Night Come* (Theatr Clwyd), *The Weavers* (costume designs - Gate Theatre), *Twelfth Night* (Central School of Speech & Drama), *The Sunset Ship* (Young Vic), *Lovers* (RSC Fringe Festival). Opera includes *A Medicine for Melancholy*, *A-Ronné* (both ENO Bayliss Programme), *Four Saints in Three Acts* (Trinity Opera), *King and Marshal* (Bloomsbury Theatre).

KEITH THOMPSON *Musician*

Studied Oboe/Piano at the Royal Academy of Music. Has worked as Music Director for the Royal National Theatre, Royal Shakespeare Company and Shakespeare's Globe. Has played in many groups and London Orchestras and was a founder member of the Michael Nyman Band. Has recorded and performed in over 30 films, most recently *The Governess*, *Elizabeth* and *Shakespeare in Love*. Most recent theatre includes *Mutability*, *The London Cuckolds* (both Royal

National Theatre) and *As You Like It* (Shakespeare's Globe and Tokyo Globe Theatre).

YASMIN WILDE *Performer*

Theatre includes *The Jungle Book*, *Arabian Nights* (both Midlands Arts Centre), *Heavenly Bodies* (Leicester Haymarket), *Shakers* (Hull Truck Theatre), *The Jungle Book* (Manchester Library Theatre), *Romeo and Juliet* (Orange Tree Theatre), *Yerma* (Southwark Playhouse), *Dancing in the Street*, *Summer in the City* (both DGM Productions). Television includes *The Talent Trial* (HTV), *The Bill* (Thames TV), *Teenage Health Freak* (Channel 4).

GARY YERSHON *Composer*

Theatre includes *The Unexpected Man*, *Hamlet* (both RSC), *Art* (West End/Broadway), *The Way of the World*, *Broken Glass*, *Volpone*, *Pericles* (all Royal National Theatre), *My Mother Said I Never Should* (Oxford Stage Company), *Hunting Scenes from Lower Bavaria* (Gate Theatre), *Doña Rosita* (Almeida). Television includes *James the Cat* (ITV). Radio includes *Room of Leaves* (BBC Radio 4).

Arabian Nights

The folk tales which have collectively survived as *The Thousand and One Nights* are of Indian, Persian, and Arabic origin. Many of the stories were circulated orally for centuries before being written down.

The first records that the tales existed orally come to us via Arab historians from the tenth century. It was only by the latter half of the thirteenth century, however, that the different manuscripts of the tales began to emerge in written form. During the eighteenth century, the first European translations began to appear, influencing writers such as Rousseau and the English Romantics, and became as much a part of Western culture as Eastern. However, Eastern scholars were reluctant to give these irreverent stories the 'classic' status they were achieving for themselves in the West.

Since the thirteenth century, there have been many versions of *The Thousand and One Nights,* mainly from Egypt and Syria. Most recent scholarship claims a fourteenth century Syrian manuscript as the authentic text, but no doubt there will be others who disagree.

What endures over and above these academic debates is the strange power of the tales themselves, with their depiction of a unique world of supernatural forces and fabulous wealth, juxtaposed with the basic physical conditions and deep-rooted psychological needs of ordinary people, whether they be medieval or contemporary, Islamic or Christian, young or old.

Craig Higginson

ARABIAN NIGHTS

adapted by
Dominic Cooke

For Aoife

Cast

The original production called for a company of nine. The parts could happily be played by the same or more actors and distributed differently. It is essential that Shahrayar is listening, and not participating in, the first few stories and preferable that there is some resonance between the casting of Envious Sisters and the Frame story. At the Young Vic the parts were divided as follows:

Actor 1. Shahrayar / Great (Abu Hassan) / Ghoul (Wife Who Wouldn't Eat) / Khosrou Shah

Actor 2. Vizier / Captain of Forty Thieves / Doctor / Es-Sindibad the Sailor / Haroun al-Rashid / Vizier (Envious Sisters) / Wise Old Man

Actor 3. Masud / Ali Baba / Little Beggar / Sidi 2 / Baker (Envious Sisters) / Perviz

Actor 4 . Headsman / Baba Mustapha / Steward / Abu Hassan / Baker (Wife Who Wouldn't Eat) / Steward (Envious Sisters)

Actor 5. Kasim / Ali Baba's Son / Tailor / Watchman / Es-Sindibad the Porter / Sidi 1 / 1st Cook / Bahman

Actress 1. Shahrazad / Chief of Police / Good Sorceress / Youngest Sister / Talking Bird

Actress 2. Dinarzad / Kasim'sWife / Tailor'sWife / Hangman / Page / 2nd Customer / Parizade

Actress 3. Shahrayar's First Wife / Marjana / Merchant (Little Beggar) / Amina / Eldest Sister / Old Religious Woman

Actress 4. Ali Baba's Wife / Doctor's Wife / King (Little Beggar) / 1st Customer / Second Sister / Steward's Wife.

Merchants in Es-Sindibad, Guests at Abu Hassan's wedding, dogs and other parts played by members of the company.

Setting: an empty space with two areas; one for storytelling and one for listening.

Prologue

SHAHRAZAD. Long long ago, in a faraway land, there lived a clever young girl called Shahrazad.

DINARZAD. She lived with her little sister who was called Dinarzad . . .

VIZIER. . . . and her father who was the Vizier, the chief adviser to the King. The Vizier loved both his daughters very much.

A family grouping.

DINARZAD. Dinarzad was as kind, loyal and true as any girl her age.

SHAHRAZAD. But Shahrazad was courageous, shrewd and bright well beyond her years. And there was nothing she liked better than to read. Shahrazad read books of literature, philosophy and medicine. She liked to read poetry, history, and the sayings of wise men and kings. But best of all she liked to read stories.

DINARZAD. Stories of enchanted caves . . .

SHAHRAZAD. . . . of flesh eating ghouls, . . .

DINARZAD. . . . of talking birds, . . .

SHAHRAZAD. . . . flying men.

DINARZAD. And night after night, she would keep her little sister awake by filling her head with these stories.

Dinarzad lies in bed with the covers pulled up high. Shahrazad sits at the end of the bed. She is in the middle of telling a terrifying story.

SHAHRAZAD. When suddenly the huge bird dropped him in a valley of slimy tree-sized snakes.

DINARZAD *screams.*

VIZIER (*enters*). It's getting very late, children, you must get to sleep.

DINARZAD. Please father, please let Shahrazad finish.

SHAHRAZAD. We're near the end now.

VIZIER. Very well then. The end of the story. Then sleep.

SHAHRAZAD. However many times she told these tales, she never forgot a word. For Shahrazad was gifted with a perfect memory.

SHAHRAYAR. Now the King of this country was called Shahrayar.

QUEEN. He lived with a beautiful wife that he loved as he loved his own eyes.

Another family grouping. They dance together, romantically.

SHAHRAYAR. Shahrayar was a great leader; courageous, big hearted and strong. By his enemies he was feared but by his people he was loved.

VIZIER. And the halls of the palace would sing with his laughter.

We see the laughing King.

SHAHRAYAR. One day Shahrayar was at the Palace window overlooking the garden, when a secret door opened.

Shahrayar watches as his wife, the queen, comes out, She looks around

QUEEN. Masud, Masud!

A slave jumps from a tree and rushes to her. They dance sensually together.

SHAHRAYAR. I trusted my wife as I trusted the ground beneath my feet. No man is safe in the world. Curse the World, curse Life and curse all Women!

VIZIER. Now the King is strengthened by his Vizier as the body is by the back.

SHAHRAYAR. Shahrayar went to the Vizier and said to him:

Take that wife of mine and put her to death.

VIZIER. The Vizier did this, for if he disobeyed the King's will he would be killed himself.

SHAHRAYAR. The gates of the King's heart were locked like a prison

VIZIER. and the halls of the palace were as silent as a tomb.

SHAHRAYAR. The King swore that from now on he would marry for one night only –

A stilted wedding dance

– and the next morning . . .

THE VIZIER. . . . . order the Vizier to have the Headsman cut off his wife's head.

SHAHRAYAR. He continued to do this for a thousand nights . . .

WOMEN. . . . . till a thousand young girls perished . . .

SHAHRAYAR. . . . . and every morning he would say to himself:

There is not a single good woman anywhere on the face of the earth.

SHAHRAZAD. By now, Shahrazad had grown up into a wise, refined, and beautiful young woman.

DINARZAD. Dinarzad had grown up too!

VIZIER. One day the Vizier returned home from the palace with his head weighed down with worry.

SHAHRAZAD. Why are you looking so lost, Father?

VIZIER. It seems the sun has set on our city forever. Mothers and daughters are fleeing in fear. And those that are left behind are locked up in their houses. Today I passed the mosque and saw hundreds of shoes lined up outside. Not one pair was a woman's.

SHAHRAZAD. Father, I have a favour to ask and hope that you will grant me it.

VIZIER. I will not refuse it. If it is just and reasonable.

SHAHRAZAD. I have a plan to save the daughters of the city.

VIZIER. Your aim, daughter is admirable but King Shahrayar's sickness is beyond help. How could you hope to cure it?

SHAHRAZAD. I want you to marry me to the King.

Silence.

I mean it father. I want you to marry me to him. Today.

VIZIER. Have you lost your mind, daughter? You know what happens in the Palace every morning.

SHAHRAZAD. I know that father. I am not afraid.

VIZIER. When the King orders me to send you to the headsman, I must obey. I, your father, will have your blood on my hands.

SHAHRAZAD. Father, you must trust me. Marry me to the King.

VIZIER. I forbid you to ever mention this again.

SHAHRAZAD. Either you take me, or I shall go myself.

VIZIER. Silence!

SHAHRAZAD. And if I go, I will tell the King that I asked you to marry me to him and you refused. That you begrudged him your daughter and disobeyed his will.

VIZIER. Please think again, daughter. Don't do this.

SHAHRAZAD. I'm sorry father, I must.

VIZIER. Tired and defeated, the Vizier went to King Shahrayar.

Vizier kisses the ground before The King.

VIZIER. He told the King about his daughter, adding that he would bring her to him that very night.

SHAHRAYAR. Vizier, how could you give me your daughter knowing that I will order you to send her to the Executioner tomorrow morning?

VIZIER. My King and Lord, I have explained all this to her, but she insists on being with you tonight.

SHAHRAYAR. You realise that if you refuse, as a matter of honour, I will put you to death as well.

VIZIER. Yes, my lord.

SHAHRAYAR. Go to her, prepare her and bring her to me early in the evening.

VIZIER. The Vizier went home and repeated the King's message to his daughter.

May Allah not deprive me of you.

SHAHRAZAD. Shahrazad was delighted and went to her younger sister.

Dinarzad, listen closely to what I have to say. When I go to the King, I will send for you to stay with me in the bridal chamber. When you come, remember to wake me an hour before daybreak and ask me to tell you a story.

DINARZAD. Sister, I will do all I can to help you.

VIZIER. At nightfall the Vizier led Shahrazad to the Palace of great King Shahrayar.

The King enters.

Shahrazad kisses the ground before the King.

A short, strained wedding ritual dance. Shahrayar and Shahrazad are left alone.

SHAHRAYAR. Uncover your face.

Shahrazad removes her veil.

You are very beautiful.

Shahrazad starts crying.

Why are you crying?

SHAHRAZAD. I have a sister. I would like her to stay with me here tonight, so that I might say good-bye and enjoy her company one last time.

SHAHRAYAR. Shahrayar agreed and Dinarzad was sent for . . .

DINARZAD. . . . who came with all possible speed.

SHAHRAYAR. The King and Queen got into a bed raised very high . . .

DINARZAD. . . . and Dinarzad lay down on some cushions on the floor underneath. An hour before daybreak, Dinarzad did as her sister asked.

Sister, if you are not too sleepy, tell me one of your strange and wonderful stories to while away the night, for I don't know what will happen to you tomorrow.

SHAHRAZAD. May I have permission to tell a story, my Lord?

SHAHRAYAR. You may.

SHAHRAZAD. Very well.

Listen . . . .

ACT ONE

The Story of Ali Baba and the Forty Thieves

In this story, the thieves are played as a chorus, becoming the horses, the cave, and the treasure inside.

SHAHRAZAD. In a city in Persia there lived two brothers, one called Kasim and the other Ali Baba. When he died, their loving father left them an equal share of his tiny fortune. But luck had not been half as fair.

KASIM. Kasim married a widow who owned a shop bursting with fine goods. He soon became a wealthy man and lived a life of ease.

ALI BABA. Ali Baba, on the other hand, married a woman as dirt poor as he was. He lived very sparsely and was forced to scratch a living chopping wood in a nearby forest and bringing it to sell in town on two asses, which were all he owned in the world.

One day, when Ali Baba was in the forest, he noticed, in the distance, a vast cloud of dust. When he looked closer he saw a band of horsemen riding towards him at great speed. Ali Baba was suspicious. He climbed a tall, close-leafed tree, next to a cliff, where he could hide without being seen.

SHAHRAZAD. The horsemen were strong and armed with knives as sharp as snake's fangs. They came to the foot of the cliff and jumped from their saddles.

ALI BABA. Ali Baba counted the men and found that they numbered forty. He guessed from their cold eyes and black beards that they were bandits. Ali Baba could see that their saddle bags were bulging with gold and silver.

CAPTAIN. The one he took for their Captain passed under the tree and stood in front of the cliff:

OPEN SESAME!

ALI BABA. No sooner had he said this than, as if by magic, a
stone door in the cliff yawned wide open.

CAPTAIN. After inspecting the band, one by one, as they went
through the door, the Captain looked darkly over his
shoulder and followed them in.

ALI BABA. Immediately the door swept shut. Ali Baba froze
in the tree for some time. Eventually, it opened again, and
the forty thieves appeared.

CAPTAIN. CLOSE, SESAME!

The door shuts.

SHAHRAZAD. Each thief mounted his horse and they
galloped off into the dust.

Ali Baba climbs down and goes to the door.

ALI BABA. OPEN SESAME.

Instantly the door flies wide open.

Ali Baba was astonished to find a bright, airy cavern, carved
out of the rock like the holy dome of a mosque. Inside was
a landscape of limitless riches. Islands of sparkling treasure
sat in rivers of rich silks and brocades, valleys of precious
carpets and above all, mountain upon mountain of sacks and
purses bursting with shimmering gold and silver coins.
He quickly gathered as many gold coins as his asses could
carry.

OPEN SESAME!

He goes through the door.

CLOSE SESAME !

The door shuts.

He covered the coins with firewood to prevent them being
seen and set off for home.

Ali Baba arrives home.

Wife, look what I have for you.

*Ali Baba puts the bags at her feet. His wife prods them,. She
looks inside one. He empties the bags on to the floor.*

ALI'S WIFE. Ali Baba, How could you? We may be poor, but there's no need to steal

ALI BABA. Shh wife. Calm down and keep quiet. Wait till you hear what just happened.

He told her his adventures from beginning to end and they agreed to keep the whole story as secret as the mystery of the pyramids.

ALI'S WIFE. We're rich !

She does a little dance of joy and then starts to count the gold piece by piece.

One, two, three, four . . . .

ALI BABA. Don't be a dolt, wife. It would take all week to get this lot counted. We need to hide the coins. This minute. I shall dig a hole in the garden.

ALI'S WIFE. No, it's no good. I simply have to know precisely how much we've got. I'll borrow some scales from the neighbours. I'll quickly weigh the gold while you dig the hole.

ALI BABA. Alright then. But remember: be on your guard.

ALI'S WIFE. Ali Baba's wife fluttered over to her brother-in-law Kasim's, who lived nearby. As he was not at home, she asked his wife if she would kindly lend her some scales for a short while.

KASIM'S WIFE. Certainly. Wait here while I fetch them.

Now, the sister-in-law knew how poor Ali Baba was, and was desperate to find out what they could be weighing. So she greased the inside of the pan of the scales.

Kasim's wife goes back and gives the scales to Ali Baba's wife.

I am sorry it's taken me so long. I couldn't find them anywhere.

ALI'S WIFE. Ali Baba's wife took the scales home and began to weigh the gold. Whilst Ali Baba buried it, she returned them, saying:

Sister in law, I said I would only be a while. I am as good as my word. Here they are. I am much obliged.

Kasim's wife peers into the scales and finds a piece of gold stuck to the pan.

KASIM'S WIFE. What is this? Ali Baba has enough gold to fill a pair of scales? Where did the penniless pauper get it from?

KASIM. Her husband Kasim was at his shop. When he came home, his wife said:

KASIM'S WIFE. Kasim, you think yourself rich, but you are mistaken, Ali Baba has far more money than you. He doesn't count his gold as you do. He weighs it.

SHAHRAZAD. She told him the trick she had played on Ali Baba's wife, and showed him the coin she had found.

KASIM. Instead of feeling happy for Ali Baba's good fortune, Kasim was stricken with deadly jealousy. Before sunrise the next morning, he marched straight over to his brother's house.

Ali Baba, my wife found this stuck to the scales you borrowed yesterday.

Kasim shows Ali Baba the coin.

I demand an explanation.

ALI BABA. Ali Baba realised that, thanks to his dozy wife, Kasim had discovered their secret. So, rather than risking the thieves' gold, he struck a deal. He agreed to tell Kasim where he found the treasure, if Kasim would share it equally and promise never to tell a soul.

KASIM. At dawn the next day, Kasim set off with ten mules loaded with huge chests that he intended to fill. He followed the directions Ali Baba had given till he got to the cliff:

OPEN SESAME !

The door flies open. As soon as he enters the cave, it snaps shut.

His eyes pored over the riches inside, which were far beyond his wildest dreams. Greed and longing so possessed him that he spent the day in open mouthed wonder, and clean forgot till evening that he had come to take some away.

At last he snapped out of his trance and dragged as many sacks as he could to the door. But when he came to open it, his head was so full of greedy daydreams that he forgot the password.

OPEN SATSUMA!

The door remains closed

OPEN SEMOLINA! . . . OPEN SULTANA! . . . OPEN SARDINE!

The stubborn door doesn't budge.

The more Kasim searched for the word, the more it escaped him, until the flame of his greed went out and froze into icy dread.

SHAHRAZAD. Towards midnight, the thieves returned to their cavern and noticed Kasim's mules grazing dozily by the rock, loaded with empty trunks.

CAPTAIN. The Captain went directly to the door, with his steely dagger glinting in his hand:

OPEN SESAME!

Kasim charges out with such force that he knocks down the captain. But he cannot escape the other thieves, who are also holding their daggers, and who kill him on the spot.

SHAHRAZAD. The thieves cut Kasim's body into quarters and displayed it inside the cavern, placing two pieces on one side of the door and two on the other. This would terrify anyone else who attempted to break in. Then, they mounted their horses, and set off to search the countryside for caravans to rob.

KASIM'S WIFE. Meanwhile, Kasim's wife was worried sick when, by nightfall, her husband hadn't returned. She hurried to Ali Baba's house:

It's late and my husband hasn't come home and I'm terrified something bad has happened.

ALI BABA. After begging her to stay calm for the sake of secrecy, Ali Baba set off for the forest with his asses. When he approached the cliff, he saw no sign of his brother or the mules. But he did see a pool of blood by the door which chilled him to the bone.

He crept to the door and gave the command. When it opened, his blood turned to ice at the sight of his brother's quartered body.

Despite Kasim's coldness towards him, Ali Baba knew that, by Allah's law, his brother must be buried properly. So without hesitating, he found a cloth to wrap up the remains. Then, he loaded them onto his asses with three more sacks of gold and set off back to his sister's house in town.

Ali Baba knocks at the door.

MARJANA. The door was opened by Marjana, a clever slave-girl, who he knew to be loyal and fearless.

ALI BABA. When he entered the courtyard he took Marjana aside.

Marjana, my life depends on your secrecy. These two bundles contain your master's murdered body. Without raising any suspicion, we must bury him as if he died of natural causes. For if anyone suspects that he was murdered, his killers will come in search of me as his accomplice.

MARJANA. The next day, Marjana went to a nearby druggist, and asked him for tablets that would cure a deadly disease.

DRUGGIST. The druggist gave her a small bottle and enquired who was ill.

MARJANA (*tearfully*). Ah, it is Kasim himself, my master. We don't know what it is, but he cannot breathe a word, nor eat a crumb. I fear that we shall lose him.

SHAHRAZAD. When neighbours watched Ali Baba and his wife going back and forth all day long with sad, downcast faces, they were not surprised to hear the heartrending cries of Kasim's wife and Marjana . . .

MARJANA. . . . who announced that Kasim was dead.

First thing the next morning, Marjana set off to visit a poor old cobbler on the market square called Baba Mustapha.

BABA. Because he was so penniless, he needed to work harder than anyone else and his shop was always the first to open.

MARJANA. Good morning

She places a gold coin in his hand.

Baba Mustapha, fetch your needle and thread and come with me quickly. But I must warn you, when we leave the town centre I shall blindfold you.

BABA. What are you up to? I don't like the sound of this. I've got my reputation to think about.

Marjana places another gold coin in his hand.

MARJANA. Your good name is safe in my hands. Just come with me and fear nothing.

BABA. Baba Mustapha followed Marjana through the morning shadows, to the edge of the town centre.

She blindfolds him.

MARJANA. She led him to Kasim's house, to the room where the quartered body lay.

She takes his blindfold off.

Baba Mustapha, I brought you here to sew the pieces of this body together. When you finish, I shall give you another piece of gold.

Baba Mustapha sews the four pieces into one. Marjana gives Baba another coin. She blindfolds him again.

Marjana forced Baba Mustapha to swear an oath of secrecy. Then she led him back to the edge of the town centre.

She takes the blindfold off.

When she returned, they carried Kasim's body to the cemetery.

KASIM'S WIFE. His wife stayed at home crying bitter tears of grief.

SHAHRAZAD. And so the secret of Kasim's gruesome murder was locked away as tight as the clasp on a miser's purse. And no one in the city suspected a thing.

ALI BABA. Three days later, under the cloak of nightfall, Ali Baba . . .

ALI'S WIFE. . . . his wife . . .

ALI'S SON. . . . and their son . . .

ALI BABA. . . . carried their few belongings . . . ,

ALI'S WIFE. . . . with their gold . . .

ALI'S SON. . . . to Kasim's big house . . .

ALL THREE. . . . to live in wealth and splendour.

ALI BABA. Ali Baba gave Kasim's thriving shop to his son . . .

Ali Baba gives his son a key.

. . . promising that if he managed it wisely, he would receive the key to greater riches when he married.

SHAHRAZAD. Let us leave Ali Baba to the fruits of his golden fortune and return to the forty thieves.

When they returned to their forest hideaway, they were astounded to find Kasim's body and several bags of gold missing.

CAPTAIN. Someone else knows the secret of the cave. We must act quickly or risk losing everything. I shall go down into the town and listen out for talk of a murdered man. I shall find out who he was and where he lived. When I find his accomplice we shall put him to a slow and lingering death.

Temptation

The King's room. Dawn.

Sound of a sword being sharpened.

SHAHRAZAD. But darkness bleeds into day, your majesty.
I hear the executioner sharpening his knife.

DINARZAD. What an extraordinary story, sister. I would love
to hear the rest of it.

SHAHRAZAD. You will never guess what happens next. I
shall tell you tonight, if the King lets me live.

Enter the Vizier.

VIZIER. The executioner awaits your command, your majesty.

SHAHRAZAD. Doesn't his majesty want to know what
happens to Ali Baba?

Pause.

And whether the cunning slave girl outwits the Captain of
the forty thieves?

Pause. Shahrayar is torn.

SHAHRAYAR. Vizier, come back tomorrow. At the same time.

VIZIER. Certainly, your majesty.

Shahrazad, Dinarzad and Vizier share a moment of relief.

SHAHRAZAD. The day melted into night.

DINARZAD. And an hour before dawn, Dinarzad said:

Sister, if you are not too sleepy, tell the rest of your strange
and wonderful story

SHAHRAZAD. May I have your permission to continue the
story, my Lord?

SHAHRAYAR. Yes.

SHAHRAZAD. Very well. Listen . . .

The Story of Ali Baba and the Forty Thieves continues

CAPTAIN. The captain of the forty thieves disguised himself and set off, arriving in the city at daybreak. He walked and walked, until he came to the first shop he saw open.

BABA. It was the shabby shop of Baba Mustapha.

Baba Mustapha sits with a needle in his hand, sewing a shoe.

CAPTAIN. Good morning old man. You start work very early. Is it possible that at your fine old age you have such good eyesight?

BABA. You do not know me. I may be old as the crumbling earth, but I still have perfect eyes. Not long ago, in a place much darker than his, I stitched up the body of a dead man.

CAPTAIN. A dead man! What do you mean? Surely you mean you stitched up the shroud that a dead man was wrapped in?

BABA. Ah. You want me to speak, but you shall know no more.

The Captain pulls out a gold coin, and puts it into Baba Mustapha's hand.

CAPTAIN. I merely ask you to do me one small favour. Show me the dead man's house.

BABA. Even if I wanted to, I couldn't. I was blindfolded. I didn't see a thing.

CAPTAIN. Come on, let me blindfold you again. We'll see if you can retrace your steps.

The Captain gives Baba Mustapha a second coin. Baba Mustapha holds the two pieces of gold in his hand, deliberating, then pockets them.

BABA. I cannot be sure that I'll remember the way exactly, but, since you are so persuasive, I will do my best.

CAPTAIN. To the great joy of the captain of the forty thieves ...

BABA. .... he stood up andled the Captain to the spot where Marjana had bound his eyes.

*The Captain blindfolds Baba Mustapha. Baba leads off,
retracing his steps.*

Baba Mustapha led the thief to Kasim's house, where Ali
Baba now lived.

CAPTAIN. Before pulling off the blindfold, the Captain
marked the front door with a cross of red chalk. Then he
sent the old man on his way and raced back to the thieves.

MARJANA. A short while later, Marjana, whose sight was as
sharp as a butcher's blade, went out of Ali Baba's house on
an errand. When she returned, seeing the red cross on the
door, she stopped to examine it.

Hmm. I don't like the look of this. I think someone may be
out to harm my master.

She took another piece of red chalk and without saying a
word to her master or mistress, marked a cross on every
other door in the street.

CAPTAIN. Meanwhile, the Captain rejoined the others in the
forest and ordered them to go down to the city in disguise.
He instructed them to gather in the street by the house with
the red cross.

SHAHRAZAD. The thieves set off in groups of two or three,
arriving at the town without anyone noticing.

CAPTAIN. When The Captain came to the street, the thieves
were milling about. He came to the first house marked with
a red cross and pointed it out.

But then he noticed that next door was marked in exactly
the same way. And when he saw a big red cross marked on
every front door in the street, he was dumfounded and
discombobulated.

Furious to see his plans foiled, he sent his men back to the
dark forest, whilst he returned to Baba Mustapha . . .

BABA. . . . who led him, as he had done before, back to Ali
Baba's house.

CAPTAIN. This time he observed the house so closely, by
walking past it many, many times, that it was impossible for

him to mistake it ever again. Contented, he returned to the forest and ordered the thieves to buy twenty mules and forty large leather jars, one full of oil and the others completely empty. He made each man, armed with their spiky dagger, climb inside a jar and loaded two jars on each mule. Then they set off for town and arrived as twilight shadows fell on Ali Baba's doorstep . . .

Captain disguises himself as an Oil Merchant..

ALI BABA. . . . where the owner was taking in some fresh evening air . . .

SON. . . . with his son.

CAPTAIN. The captain stopped his mules and said:

Sir, my name is Kawaja Husain. I have brought some oil from a faraway place, to sell at market tomorrow. Would it be possible to spend the night under your roof?

ALI BABA. Ali Baba didn't recognise the Captain through his disguise.

Welcome!

CAPTAIN. Kawaja Husain, or rather the Captain of the forty thieves, unloaded the jars. He went from jar to jar saying:

Have your daggers at the ready. When the time is right I shall return and give the signal.

After this, he went back into the house, to join Ali Baba for supper.

MARJANA. Marjana set about preparing a rich, tasty meal. While she was cooking, the oil lamp in the kitchen went out and there were no candles or oil to be found in the house. So, she picked up the oil pot and went into the yard to borrow some from one of the forty jars. When she drew close to the first jar . . .

SHAHRAZAD. . . . the thief inside whispered:

Is it time yet?

MARJANA. Any other slave but Marjana would have bleated
like a goat. But she was above that. Without so much as a
twitch, she replied:

Not yet. But soon.

Jar by jar she went round quietly, giving the same answer,
until she came to the jar filled with oil.

This way, Marjana learned that there were forty vengeful
thieves in the house and that this so-called oil merchant was
their captain.

She filled her oil pot and hurried to the kitchen. As soon as
she had lit the lamp, she took the biggest pan in the house
and went back to the courtyard. She filled it to the brim
with thick, gloopy oil and coming back to the kitchen set it
onto a crackling fire. As soon as it bubbled and spat, she
picked it up, took it out, pouring enough of the scalding oil
into each jar to choke every thief and kill him.

Marjana kills the thieves in the jars.

When she had done this, she went with the slave Abd Allah
to serve the food and wine.

Abd Allah serves plates

Marjana serves wine with three wine cups.

CAPTAIN. Just then, the captain hatched a bloodthirsty scheme.

There's no need to call my men, he thought.

It will give me great pleasure to deal with this cockroach
myself. I will get them both drunk, so they fall asleep.
Then, I shall slice my enemy in two like a ripe watermelon.

MARJANA.. However, Marjana had spotted the Captain of the
Forty Thieves' knife through his clothes and knew what he
was up to. She went to Abd Allah:

Fetch your tambourine. Let's go and entertain our master,
his son and guest.

*She puts on a dancer's head-dress and veil. Abd Allah plays
his tambourine and walks before Marjana into the hall.*

Marjana bows deeply.

ALI BABA. Come in Marjana. Kawaja Husain will tell us what he thinks of your performance.

Abd Allah starts to play and sing.

Marjana pulls out the dagger and performs a hugely energetic, mesmerising, sometimes violent dance in which she thrusts the dagger both inwards and outward. Eventually she snatches the tambourine from Abd Allah with her left hand, and holding the dagger in her right, presents the tambourine as if to collect money.

Ali Baba and his son put a piece of gold in. The Captain pulls his purse out but as he puts his hand in, Marjana plunges the dagger into his heart.

ALI BABA. Wretched woman, what have you done? You've ruined us all.

MARJANA. I did this to save you, not ruin you. Look here.

She goes to take out the captain's dagger and shows it to Ali Baba

See what an enemy you had within your gates. Look closely and you shall see the captain of the forty thieves.

MARJANA. Marjana told him all that she had done, from the first noticing the cross on the door, to the destruction of the thieves and their captain.

ALI BABA. When Marjana finished, Ali Baba was struck by her courage and quick-wittedness.

I owe my life to you. To show my thanks I give you your freedom from this moment and if he will agree, my son's hand in marriage.

SON. Far from refusing, his son was delighted.

SON AND MARJANA. and a few days later, with a sacred blessing and an extravagant feast, they were married.

*Short wedding tableau that echoes Shahrayar and
Shahrazad, except this time full of joy and light. Just as the
married couple kiss, Shahrayar interrupts and the
'characters' scatter.*

Threat

The King's room. Dawn.

Sound of a sword being sharpened.

SHAHRAYAR. So you think he was happy? This son of Ali
    Baba?

SHAHRAZAD. So the story goes.

SHAHRAYAR. He marries a crafty, cunning woman and lives
    in a fine house. He is sure to be tricked and lied to and
    broken in two by this scheming slavegirl.

SHAHRAZAD. My lord, the story says otherwise.

SHAHRAYAR. Your story is written by a liar.

    Enter Vizier

VIZIER. The executioner is waiting outside, my lord.

DINARZAD. I know you have many other tales, sister.
    Perhaps you could tell us one tonight.

SHAHRAYAR. I have no more time to listen to your sister's
    prattling. Executioner!

SHAHRAZAD. What a shame, for tonight I would have told
    you the intriguing tale of . . . Forgive me, my lord, I speak
    out of turn.

    Enter Executioner.

SHAHRAYAR. Executioner, take her away.

    Executioner grabs her and leads her out.

    One word. Before you go.

They stop.

What was the name of the story you were going to tell me?

SHAHRAZAD. The Story of The Little Beggar.

SHAHRAYAR. What sort of story is it?

SHAHRAZAD. One to put a smile on a King's face.

SHAHRAYAR. Laughter died with my first wife.

SHAHRAZAD. The King in this story finds laughter where he least expects it.

SHAHRAYAR. I have a mind to hear it. You shall tell me tonight. Tomorrow, Vizier.

Vizier signals to the Headsman to let Shahrazad go.

Shahrazad, Dinarzad and Vizier share a moment of relief.

Exit Vizier and Headsman.

SHAHRAZAD. The day melted into night.

DINARZAD. And an hour before dawn, Dinarzad said:

Sister, if you are not too sleepy, tell us another strange and wonderful story.

SHAHRAZAD. May I tell my story, my Lord?

SHAHRAYAR. You may.

SHAHRAZAD. Very well.

Listen . . .

The Story of the Little Beggar

A raised area with steps is required for this story. This might be a ladder or a moveable platform. It acts as the doctor's house, chimney and scaffold.

SHAHRAZAD. Once there lived a tailor, with a pretty and faithful wife. One day while taking a walk, they bumped into a jolly little beggar.

He is smartly dressed with a scarf and a tall green hat, improvising a slapstick death routine with singing and tambourine. The tailor and wife laugh and clap.

TAILOR. When they got close they could smell wine on his breath and realised that he was roaring drunk.

He puts his tambourine under his arm and claps his hands in time with his song:

BEGGAR.
If you fancy cheering up
Feed my belly and fill my cup!

TAILOR. The tailor and his wife took so strongly to the Little Beggar that they asked him to come home with them to eat.

TAILOR'S WIFE. He accepted and went with them back to their house.

TAILOR AND TAILOR'S WIFE. They all sat down to a delicious meal of bread and fish.

TAILOR. They ate and drank till they had finished everything . . .

TAILOR'S WIFE. . . . except for one large fish.

TAILOR. Then, as a joke, the tailor pointed to the fish and challenged the little beggar:

I bet you can't swallow this whole.

He tries to swallow it.

TAILOR'S WIFE. But a sharp piece of bone got stuck in his throat.

He starts choking and falls to the floor. The tailor and wife, clap and laugh thinking it is an act, till his body is still. They prod him. They check him. He is stone dead.

Silence.

Don't just sit there. Do something.

TAILOR. What can I do?

TAILOR'S WIFE. Cover him with a sheet, pick him up and follow me.

TAILOR. The tailor did as his wife said . . .

TAILOR'S WIFE. . . . . and she led the way, through the streets, wailing and shrieking:

My child, my child, I pray that you will be cured of this smallpox. Why you, my child, why you?

PASSER-BY. And passers-by exclaimed:

Poor woman. Her child is ill with smallpox.

TAILOR'S WIFE. Soon they arrived at the house of a doctor.

They go up some stairs.

The wife knocks at the door.

MAID. A maid answered.

Tailor's wife hands the maid a coin.

TAILOR'S WIFE. Miss, please give this to your master. Ask him to come to see my child who is dangerously ill.

The maid goes to fetch the doctor.

Put down the beggar and run.

They rest the body in the doorway and run off.

MAID. Master, there is a sick child with its parents downstairs. They gave me a quarter piece of gold for you.

DOCTOR. Light, light, quickly, girl, quickly.

He rushes through in the dark and accidentally kicks the corpse down the stairs.

The maid comes with a candle. The doctor takes an arm and feels the pulse. Nothing.

I am finished. I have killed the patient I was supposed to cure. How will I get this body out of my house?

So he carried the little beggar upstairs to his wife and told her what had happened.

DOCTOR'S WIFE. You're neither use nor ornament! What are you sitting there for with a face like a bottle of warts? If the day breaks and he is still here, they will hang us as murderers. You must throw him down the chimney of our next-door neighbour, the King's Steward. The cats and dogs often eat his larder clean of meat and butter. Perhaps they will eat up this body.

The doctor and his wife carry the little beggar to the top of the platform and drop him through a trap or over the side. The little beggar lands on his feet. He stands, still wrapped in his blanket, bolt upright, leaning against a wall.

STEWARD. Just then, the King's Steward came home.

He opens the door, with a candle in his hand, and sees the body.

What's this? A burglar? So it's not the cats and dogs who have been eating my meat and butter, it's a man.

He picks up a stick and cracks it over the little beggar. The little beggar falls. He gives him another blow on the back. He prods him. And again. Lifts up his eyelids and realises he is dead.

What have I done? Curses on my meat and butter!

He puts the Beggar on his back.

So he carried the Little Beggar to the marketplace and leaned him up against a shop.

Again, he stands upright.

MERCHANT. At that moment, a wealthy merchant, the King's Broker, staggered by in a drunken stupor.

He stands against the wall next to (but without noticing) the Little Beggar and relieves himself. In his drunkenness, he sways into the corpse, which falls onto the Merchant's back with arms round the Merchant's neck..

Thief! Thief! Watchman! Help me!

The Merchant throws the Little Beggar to the floor with a sharp blow and begins pummelling and choking him.

WATCHMAN (*enters*) What is it?

MERCHANT. Ah Watchman, this man tried to rob me.

Watchman checks the Little Beggar to see if he is breathing and listens to his chest.

WATCHMAN. You've killed him. You're coming with me.

He grabs the Merchant and ties him up.

WATCHMAN. The Watchman took him to the Chief of Police . . .

CHIEF. . . . who threw him in a cell and, next morning, went to tell the King . . .

THE KING. . . . who ordered the merchant to be hanged.

CHIEF. And the Chief went to the Hangman . . .

HANGMAN. . . . who set up a gallows and announced the execution.

Public execution. The Merchant stands on the platform. The Hangman places noose around his neck. Drum roll.

STEWARD (*from the audience*) Stop. This man is not guilty. I am to blame for his death.

CHIEF. What did you say?

STEWARD. I am to blame for his death.

And the Steward told how he hit the Little Beggar with a stick.

Is it not enough that I have killed one man, without causing the death of another? Hang me instead.

CHIEF. Release the Merchant. Hang this man instead.

The Hangman takes the noose off the Merchant who steps down from the box. The Steward stands on the platform. The Hangman places the noose around his neck. Drum roll.

DOCTOR (*from the audience*). Stop. This man is innocent. The guilt lies at my door.

And the Doctor told how he had kicked the Little Beggar down the stairs.

Is it not enough having killed one man without causing the death of another? Hang me instead.

CHIEF. Release the Merchant and hang the Doctor.

The Hangman takes the noose off the Merchant who steps down from the platform. The Doctor stands on the platform. The Hangman places the noose around his neck. Drum roll.

TAILOR (*from the audience*). Stop. This man didn't kill the Little Beggar. No one killed him but me.

And the Tailor told how he had choked the Little Beggar with a fishbone and left the body at the Doctor's house.

When the Doctor came down, he tripped on the body of the Little Beggar and thought that he had killed him. (*To the Doctor.*) Isn't that what happened?

DOCTOR. Yes, that's right. But –

TAILOR. Release the doctor and hang me instead.

CHIEF. I've never heard the like. Release the Doctor and hang the Tailor.

The Hangman starts to take the noose off the Doctor who steps down from the platform.

DOCTOR. But –

CHIEF. Any more interruptions and I'll hang the lot of you.

DOCTOR. But . . .

CHIEF. WHAT IS IT?

DOCTOR. This body is still breathing.

All turn to look at the Little Beggar's body. There is a strange choking sound. The doctor opens his bag and takes out a giant pair of tweezers, opens the Little Beggar's mouth and puts them down his throat pulling out a huge fishbone.

BEGGAR (*huge sneeze. stands bolt upright*).
If you fancy cheering up
Feed my belly and fill my cup!

TAILOR. And word reached the King . . .

DOCTOR. . . . of the extraordinary tale of the Little Beggar's death . . .

STEWARD. . . . and the even more remarkable tale . . .

MERCHANT. . . . of his recovery.

KING. And the King sent for the Tailor, the Doctor, the Steward, the Merchant, the Little Beggar and the Chief of Police.

They all kiss the ground before him.

CHIEF. The Chief of Police told him the whole story from start to finish.

KING. I've never heard a more extraordinary story in my life.

And the King was so delighted that he awarded robes of honour . . .

TAILOR. . . . to the Tailor . . .

Tailor steps forward to receive his robe.

DOCTOR . . . Doctor . . .

Doctor steps forward to receive his robe.

STEWARD. . . . Steward . . .

Steward steps forward to receive his robe.

MERCHANT. . . . and Merchant . . .

Merchant steps forward to receive his robe.

KING. . . . and sent them on their way thanking them for entertaining him with such an excellent story.

BEGGAR. And the Little Beggar was appointed the King's jester . . .

SHAHRAZAD. . . . and made the King chuckle for the rest of his days.

King starts smiling, giggles, then a loud laugh cracks though him.

Warning

The King's room. Dawn.

Sound of a sword being sharpened.

SHAHRAZAD. The darkness is lifting, your majesty.

SHAHRAYAR. This laughing King is a fool like I once was, before I learned the truth about women. Laughter should be a stranger to a King's heart.

Enter Vizier.

VIZIER. What shall I tell the executioner, my lord?

DINARZAD. I would love to hear another of your wonderful stories tonight.

SHAHRAZAD. I will tell you one. An extraordinary tale of adventure and survival against all odds. If the King spares my life.

SHAHRAYAR. Do you take me for a fool, woman?

SHAHRAZAD. I know you to be the wisest of men, my lord.

SHAHRAYAR. Then why do you think you can trick me?

SHAHRAZAD. Trick you, your majesty?

SHAHRAYAR. Trying to tempt me with your senseless stories!

SHAHRAZAD. If you feel you are being tricked, Good King, I shall never breathe a word of a story again.

SHAHRAYAR. I will be the one to decide that.

SHAHRAZAD. Yes, my lord.

SHAHRAYAR. I hear your stories as and when I choose. And when I no longer choose, you will die like the others.

SHAHRAZAD. As your majesty pleases.

SHAHRAYAR. Vizier, you may go.

Shahrazad, Dinarzad and Vizier share a moment of relief.

SHAHRAZAD. The day melted into night.

DINARZAD. And an hour before dawn, Dinarzad said:

> Sister, if you are not too sleepy, tell us another strange and
> wonderful story.

SHAHRAZAD. May I, my Lord?

SHAHRAYAR. Go on.

SHAHRAZAD. Very well.

> Listen . . .

The Story of Es-Sindibad the Sailor

*Es-Sindibad the Sailor uses a puppet of his younger self to act
out much of his story. The rest of the images are created by the
company using masks, models and puppets.*

SHAHRAZAD. Once, in the city of Baghdad, there lived a
poor man who earned his living by carrying loads on his
head. He was called Es-Sindibad the Porter.

One day, as he was staggering under a heavy load in the
sweltering heat of the summer sun, he stopped to rest.

He puts down his load and looks around.

PORTER. He found himsef in a shaded spot by a fine
merchant's house. The ground before it was swept and
watered. A cool and fragrant breeze blew through the
doorway, and from within came the sweet strains of a lute.

Es-Sindibad the Porter begins his s ong.

PORTER. Heavy my burden and desperate my state,
Forsaken by fortune, cursed by fate.
Others are wealthy and charmed is their life.
Shielded from worry, sheltered from strife.

Many men toil in the sun to get paid.
Whilst others they rest and recline in the shade.

All Allah's creatures live under one sun
Our bodies are equal, Our souls are as one.
Yet some men live poor lives, others live fine,
One scrimps for vinegar, one sips on wine.

Many men toil in the sun to get paid.
Whilst others they rest and recline in the shade.

He finishes the song and places his load on his head.

PORTER. Just as he was about to go on his way . . .

PAGE. . . . a smartly dressed page appeared.

The Page takes him by the hand.

Please come in. My master would like to speak with you.

PORTER. The porter politely declined . . .

PAGE. . . . but the page would would not be deterred.

PORTER. So Es-Sindbad left his load at the door and followed
the page into the house.

He was led into a magnificent and spacious hall, as golden
as the palace of a King. At one end sat a distinguished old
man whose beard was touched with silver.

Es-Sindibad the porter kisses the ground before his host.

SAILOR. You are welcome, my friend. May this day bring you
joy. What is your name and what do you do?

PORTER. My name is Es-Sindibad. By trade a porter.

SAILOR. How strange! For my name is also Es-Sindibad.
They call me Es-Sindibad the Sailor. I heard your song.

PORTER. Please don't reproach me, sir. Poverty and hardship
teach a man bad manners.

SAILOR. Do not be ashamed, for you have become a brother
to me. I found your song delightful.

Porter, I should like to tell you the story of how I came to
sit where you see me now. For my wealth was not won
without huge effort, much pain and grave, grave danger.

He indicates for the porter to sit. The porter sits.

Know this. My father was the owner of untold wealth and
property. He died when I was a little boy and left it all to
me. When I was a young man, I ate and drank freely, wore
fine clothes and frittered my days away chatting and joking
with friends, as if my wealth would last forever. By the time

I came to my senses, I found that my money was spent and I was ruined.

I was seized by horror and fear. How on earth was I going to survive? In a trice, the answer came to me. I would see the world and not come back to Baghdad until I had made my fortune. So, I sold all my possessions, put my best foot forward and boarded a ship with a group of merchants bound for the golden city of El-Basrah.

One of the company brings on the model of the ship which circles Es-Sindibad as in a memory or dream.

We passed from island to island, from sea to sea, from country to country and bought and sold and bargained until we came to a beautiful island. It was rich with leafy trees, mellow fruits, fragrant flowers, singing birds and crystal water. But there was not a soul to be seen.

Es-Sindibad starts using the puppet to tell his story.

I sat in the shade by a soothing stream. I ate my food and sipped on some wine. The air was heavy with the musk of wild flowers and before long I had drifted into a deep, deep sleep.

I cannot tell how long I slept, but when I awoke, the other passengers had gone. The ship had sailed with everyone on board, and no one remembered me. I raced frantically to the beach and looked out across the sea. There was the boat, a white speck in the vast blue ocean, dissolving into the distance.

Broken with terror and despair I collapsed on the sand. I wailed. I beat my chest. I cursed myself a thousand times for leaving Baghdad. For I was all alone without a crumb to eat or a thing to my name. I thought I was going mad.

The puppet of Es-Sindibad climbs a tree and gazes from left to right.

All I could see was sky and water and trees and birds and islands and sand. But when I scanned the island more closely, I noticed, to my surprise, a strange white object looming in the distance.

Es-Sindibad approaches the dome.

I walked round it. I could find no door. Because the surface was smooth and sleek, I couldn't climb up. I marked the spot where I stood and circled the dome once more to measure it. It was a full fifty paces. I stood there puzzling over how to get inside, when suddenly the sky turned black.

I lifted my eyes and saw a gigantic bird with a bulky body and wings as wide as terror hovering above me and blocking out the sun. In a flash I was reminded of a story I had once heard from an adventurer. In a faraway island there lives a bird of monstrous size called a Rukh, which feeds its young on elephants. Instantly, I realised that this dome was none other than a Rukh's egg.

The bird, played by several members of the company, lands on the egg and falls asleep. Es-Sindibad creeps close and stands by one of its legs.

When The Rukh was fast asleep, I sprung into action. Cunningly, I unwound my turban and twisted it like a rope. Then, I tied it around the bird's foot, saying to myself,

Praise be to Allah. This bird will carry me out of here, to civilisation.

Daybreak. The bird wakes up, screeches loudly and flies, carrying the puppet of Es Sindibad up to the sky, soaring higher and higher. It slowly swoops into land. One of the company have taken away the egg. A snake lies on the ground.

As soon as I reached the ground, I quickly loosened my turban from the Rukh's feet. Without the bird noticing, and shaking with fear, I sneakily slipped away. Then, before soaring off into the sky, it grabbed something from the ground in its talons. My heart stopped when I saw what it was holding. It was a giant serpent.

The puppet looks up and around.

I found myself at the base of a valley as deep as dread, surrounded by mountains so high, they stabbed the clouds like spears.

I am a fool, an idiot, a moron. Why didn't I stay on the island? I asked myself..

At least there was fruit to eat and water to drink. Here there is nothing. No sooner do I save myself from one peril than I plunge myself into a worse one!

I walked around the valley and was staggered to find that the ground was covered with priceless diamonds. The entire valley blazed in glorious light. To my horror, here and there amongst the shimmering stones, were coils of deadly snakes, each large enough to swallow a camel. They were slithering back to their darkened dens. For, in daylight, they hid in fear of being carried away by rukhs and eagles and eaten. They only came sliming out of their pits at night.

Consumed by terror and weak with hunger, I roamed the valley all day, searching for somewhere safe to spend the night. At dusk, I found a narrow cave. I crawled in and wedged the entrance with a small rock. But when I turned around I saw a huge snake oozing and hissing over its eggs. I leaped out of my skin. Transfixed with terror, I prayed to Allah to spare me and spent the rest of the night keeping watch. At dawn, I staggered out into the hot valley, drunk with starvation, exhaustion and fear. Suddenly, something fell out of the sky an d landed smack bang in front of me with a loud thud. It was a joint of lamb!

I was baffled, for there was not a soul in sight. Who or what could have thrown this meat? Quick as a wink, it came to me. I recalled a story I had once heard from travellers who had visited the valley of the diamonds. It is a place too dangerous to enter. But some crafty merchants have hit upon a wily scheme to gather jewels from the valley floor. At dawn, they would take a sheep, kill it, cut it up, and throw the pieces from the top of the mountain into the valley. The meat is fresh and moist and the diamonds stick to it. At midday, they wait until Eagles swoop down, pick up the meat and lift it away in their talons to their nests at the top of the mountain. With a mighty din, the merchants would rush at the birds. This would scare the eagles away, leaving the meat in the nest and the diamonds for the merchants.

Till that moment I truly believed I would never leave this valley alive. But at a stroke, I started to see a way out.

Not wishing to waste the riches at my feet, I gathered as many of the biggest diamonds I could find. I stuffed my pockets, my clothes, even my shoes to bursting.

Then, I took the cloth of my turban, twisted it, as I had before and bound myself firmly to the piece of meat. Then, I lay on the ground on my back. I put the meat on my chest and held on for dear life.

An eagle, played by one of the company, enters, swoops down, grabs the meat between its talons and soars up into the air, with Es-Sindibad clinging on for dear life. The eagle lands in its nest. Enter another puppet, The Merchant, shouting and clattering wood. The eagle flies away in fear and Es-Sindibad frees himself from the meat and stands by its side. The merchant who had been shouting comes to inspect the slaughtered sheep. He doesn't see Es-Sindibad.

MERCHANT. No diamonds? What a catastrophe! However could that have happened?

SAILOR. Hello, friend.

MERCHANT. Who are you? What the devil are you doing here?

SAILOR. Do not be alarmed, sir. I am an honest man, a sailor by profession. My story is extraordinary, and the adventure that has brought me to these mountains is more strange and wonderful than has ever been heard before. But first, please accept some of these diamonds, which I myself gathered in the valley below.

He gives the merchant some diamonds.

SAILOR. These will bring you all the riches you could wish for.

MERCHANT. A thousand thanks, good man.

SAILOR. When the other merchants heard me talking to their friend, they trooped over.

Three other merchant puppets come over.

They greeted and congratulated me on my remarkable escape and took me with them. I told them my story.

MERCHANT 2. Allah has granted you a charmed life. For no-one has set foot in the valley and come out alive.

MERCHANT 3. Allah be praised

SAILOR. They gave me food and drink and I slept soundly for many hours.

At daybreak, we set off on our journey over the great mountains together. Then we set sail and I exchanged some of my diamonds for rich merchandise and supplies including a magic antern and a flying carpet.

We traded from port to port and island to island till finally we reached Baghdad, the City of Peace.

Loaded with diamonds, coins and fragrant spices, I arrived home. I rejoiced to see my family and friends and gave gifts to them and alms to the poor. From near and far, people came to hear of my adventures and the strange sights I had seen. All were astounded at my narrow escape and wished me joy at my return from the terrors of the valley of the diamonds.

SHAHRAZAD. When Es-Sindibad had finished telling his story, he gave Es-Sindibad the Porter a hundred pieces of gold, which he took with thanks and blessings and departed.

The porter returned many times to the house of his illustrious friend, to hear more of his adventures, and the two lived in friendship for the rest of their lives.

Dawn

The King's bedroom. Dawn.

Sound of a sword being sharpened.

SHAHRAYAR. This sailor seems to survive every danger he faces.

SHAHRAZAD. Allah has blessed him with the gift of cunning, your majesty.

Enter Vizier expectantly.

SHAHRAYAR. Word has reached me, Shahrazad, that the people are praising your name for saving their daughters over these last few weeks. You are quite a heroine. Are you proud of yourself?

SHAHRAZAD. If I please the people, then I please the King, as King and people are one.

SHAHRAYAR. I hope for the people's sake that the well of your stories does not dry up.

SHAHRAZAD. Yes, my lord.

SHAHRAYAR. For I have given my word.

SHAHRAZAD. And a King's word is as precious as water.

SHAHRAYAR. Well aren't you afraid?

SHAHRAZAD. I may be afraid of dying. But not of death. I have been blessed with a life filled with joy. I would rather have short joyful life than a long life in the darkness. Life without joy is a living death.

Pause.

Shahrayar nods to Vizier.

Shahrazad, Dinarzad and Vizier share a moment of relief.

Vizier goes.

SHAHRAZAD. The day melted into night.

DINARZAD. And an hour before dawn, Dinarzad said:

Sister, if you are not too sleepy, tell us another of you strange and wonderful stories.

SHAHRAZAD. My Lord?

SHAHRAYAR. Certainly.

SHAHRAZAD. Very well.

Listen . . .

How Abu Hassan Broke Wind

SHAHRAZAD. It is said that in the city of Kaukaban in
Yemen there was a man who was the wealthiest of
merchants called Abu Hassan. His wife had died when she
was very young and his friends were always pressing him to
marry again.

ABU. So, weary of being nagged, Abu Hassan approached an
old woman . . .

MARRIAGE BROKER. . . . a marriage-broker . . .

WIFE. . . . who found him a wife with eyes as dark as a desert
night and a face as fresh as the dawn.

ABU. He arranged a sumptuous wedding banquet and
invited . . .

UNCLE AND AUNT. . . . uncles and aunts . . .

PREACHER. . . . preachers and fakirs . . .

FRIEND AND FOE. . . . friends and foes . . .

Shahrayar now joins the world of the stories as a guest.

GREAT AND GOOD. . . . and the great and the good from all
around.

ALL. The whole house was thrown open for feasting.

UNCLE AND AUNT. There was rice of five colours . . .

PREACHER. . . . sherbets of many more . . .

FRIEND. . . . goats stuffed with walnuts . . .

FOE. . . . and almonds and pistachios . . .

GREAT AND GOOD. . . . and a whole roast camel . . .

ALL. So they ate and drank and made merry . . .

BRIDE. . . . and the bride was displayed, as is the custom, in
her seven dresses to the women . . .

WOMEN. . . . who couldn't take their eyes off her.

ABU HASSAN. At last, the bridegroom was summoned to go

up to his wife . . .

WIFE. . . . who sat on a golden throne . . .

ABU HASSAN. . . . and he rose with stately dignity from the sofa. When all of a sudden he let fly a huge and deafening fart . . .

We hear a deafening fart.

AUNT. Immediately each guest turned to his neighbour . . .

FAKIR. . . . and busied himself in pressing conversation as if his life depended on it.

ABU HASSAN. But a fire of shame was lit in Abu Hassan's heart. So he excused himself and instead of going to his wife, went down to the stables, saddled his horse and rode off weeping bitter tears through the blackness of the night.

In time he reached Lahej where he boarded a ship bound for India and landed in Calicut on the Malabar coast. Here he met with many fellow Arabs who introduced him to the King.

KING. And this King trusted him and made him captain of his bodyguard.

ABU HASSAN. After ten years of peace and well-being he longed to see his home land like a lost child longs for its mother. The homesickness was so great that he thought he would die of it. So, without taking leave of the King, he set off and landed at Makalla of Hazramaut. Here, he disguised himself as a preacher and continued his journey to Kaukaban on foot suffering a hundred hardships of hunger, thirst and fatigue and braving a thousand dangers from the lion . . .

LION. . . . GRRRR . . .

ABU. . . . the snake . . .

SNAKE. . . . Hssss . . .

ABU. . . . and the ghoul . . . .

GHOUL. . . . Arrr!

ABU. By and by he reached the hill that overlook his home town. His eyes burned with tears when he saw his old house and he said to himself:

I pray no-one recognises me. I shall wonder round the outskirts and listen to the people's gossip. Allah grant no one remembers my shameful deed.

He trudged around for seven days and seven nights, until he found himself sitting on the doorstep of a hut. From inside, he heard the voice of a young girl.

GIRL. Mother, tell me what day I was born. One of my friends wants to tell my fortune.

MOTHER. You were born on the very night that Abu Hassan did his famous fart.

ABU. No sooner had he heard this than he jumped up from the step and hurried away.

SHAHRAZAD. And he didn't stop travelling till he arrived back in India, where he remained for the rest of his days.

Awakening

The King's room. Dawn.

Shahrayar has turned his back on Shahrazad. Shahrayar is smiling.

SHAHRAZAD. Did you enjoy the story, my lord.?

Shahrayar giggles, then laughs, then a huge bellyaching laugh rips out of him. Dinarzad and Shahrazad start laughing too.

Enter Vizier.   He stares at the King, bemused.

Lights fade to a solo spot on the laughing King.

Blackout.

Interval.

ACT TWO

The Story of the Wife Who Wouldn't Eat

Sidi 1 tells this story to Haroun and Sidi 2 acts it out in flashback. They are identifiable as the same person by distinctive items of the same clothing.

SHAHRAZAD. The great caliph Haroun Al-Rashid often went out into the city of Baghdad in disguise, to find out more about the lives of his people. Once, on such a trip, he saw a huge crowd of spectators in the market square.

Sidi 1 enters, riding and whipping a horse, played by the same actress who plays Amina.

They were watching a handsome young man ride a horse at full speed. He was whipping her so harshly that she was wrapped in ribbons of blood.

The Caliph was shocked by the young man's cruelty, and he asked his loyal Vizier to summon the young man to the palace. The following day, the young man came and kissed the ground before Haroun Al-Rashid. The Caliph asked his name.

SIDI 1. Sidi Nu'uman.

HAROUN. I have seen horses trained all my life, Sidi Nu'uman, but never, I am glad to say, in such a cruel, heartless way as you did yesterday. The spectators were horrified and so was I. In front of me now, you do not seem such a fearsome man, yet I am told, you do the same brutal thing every day. I would like to know the cause and have called you here today to give me a full and thorough explanation.

SIDI 1. I – I . . . .

HAROUN. Speak freely.

SIDI 1. I dare say that the way I treat my horse may seem cruel and heartless. I hope that when you hear the reasons why, you will think better of me, and see that I am more worthy of pity than blame.

HAROUN. Tell me your story.

SIDI 1. As is our country's custom, I married having never seen or met my wife. When she took off her veil after our wedding, I was pleased. I had feared she might be old, ugly and wrinkled but she seemed charming.

We see Sidi 2 unveil Amina. She lays out two plates of rice.

The day after our wedding, I sat down to lunch. My new wife was nowhere to be seen. I sent for her, and after she had kept me waiting a long, long time, she appeared.

I hid my irritation behind a polite smile. We sat down and I began to eat my rice, as usual, heartily, with a spoon,

As he speaks we see this.

My wife, however, pushed her spoon aside.

Amina pulls a little case out of her pocket. She opens it and takes out a small pair of tweezers. She uses these to pick up the rice and nibble at it, grain by grain.

Young Sidi watches her, agog. She eats politely, as if this was the proper thing to do.

Suprised at this, I said to her:

SIDI 2. Amina . . .

SIDI 1. . . . for that was her name . . .

SIDI 2. . . . Is it a family tradition of yours to eat your rice so daintily or do you have a small appetite?

Amina continues eating with the tweezers.

If you are doing it to save money, then don't worry, I promise we could afford ten thousand plates of rice and still have money to spare. Don't hold back, my dear Amina, but enjoy your food as I do.

SIDI 1. My politeness and patience fell on deaf ears.

She continues to eat slowly, grain by grain.

Her stubbornness infuriated me but I tried to excuse it.
Perhaps she was uncomfortable eating with men, perhaps
she had taken a late breakfast, perhaps she didn't like rice.
These thoughts put my mind at rest and I left her alone,
courteously.

But, the following night, at supper, she did exactly the same
thing. And the next night and the next. In fact every single
meal after that, no matter what she was served, she would
pluck and peck and nibble, eating barely enough to feed a
sparrow.

I knew it was impossible for anyone to live on so little food.
So, I decided to get to the bottom of this mystery.

One night when Amina thought me fast asleep

Sidi 2 acts out the following.

she slithered softly out of bed. I pretended to keep my eyes
shut but secretly was watching her like a hungry hawk.

She dresses and tiptoes out of the room.

The moment she turned her back, I got up, put on my robe
and went to the window. There she was, sneaking into the
street.

I ran down to the front door, which she had left half open
and followed her by the eerie light of the moon, to a nearby
graveyard. I hid behind the wall and peeked over and I saw
Amina with a ghoul.

I watched with horror as they dug up a body that had been
buried that day, cut the flesh into several pieces and ate it
up, slavering and slobbering over their sickening feast in a
way that makes me shudder to think about.

As they were filling up the grave with earth, I hurried home,
taking care to leave the door as I found it.

*Sidi 2 goes to bed. As Amina approaches, he feigns sleep.
She gets into bed beside him.*

Amina belches.

It was horrible to lie next to someone guilty of such a wicked deed, and I lay stiffly awake thinking of how I could stop this evil. I decided to put angry thoughts aside and to persuade her gently to change her ways.

The next day, at dinner, she started to eat in her usual way.

They eat together as before, Amina again eats with tweezers.

SIDI 2. You remember Amina, how surprised I was when I first saw you eat your food in such a strange and sparing fashion.

I'm sure you also remember how I urged you to taste some of the many meats which I had flavoured and prepared several different ways to please you. It seems that none of my efforts have paid off, for still you pick at your food in the same curious way. I have never lost my temper and would be sorry now to make you uneasy but tell me, Amina, dearest, does the food at my table not taste better than dead flesh?

SIDI 1. It was then that I learned that Amina was an evil sorceress.

Amina dips her hand into a basin of water and throws it into Sidi 2's face with the words

AMINA.
By the power of water drawn from a bog
Nosy wretch turn into a dog!

Sidi 2 becomes a dog and yaps pathetically at Amina. She grabs a stick and chases him with it, beating him. He outruns her. She grabs his tail meanly. He whimpers and nips her. He runs off barking and howling.

SIDI 1. Before long, all the local stray dogs were chasing after me.

Chase sequence, Whole company as dogs chasing Sidi Nu'uman through the audience and biting him where possible.

I took refuge in the doorway of a baker's who was cheerful and kind.

BAKER. Hello Dog.

The baker throws Sidi 2 a piece of bread. He licks the baker's face and wags his tail to show his appreciation. The baker laughs. Sidi then eats the piece of bread.

SIDI 1. The baker let me stay in the shop and gave me a place to sleep.

Whenever he ate breakfast, lunch or supper he always fed me scraps from the table. I loved him and was faithful and loyal at all times.

BAKER. . . . Chance! . . .

SIDI 1. . . . which was the name he gave me.

BAKER. Chance!!

Sidi 2 comes scooting in and jumps and flies up to his master, running round and round, being a playful obedient dog.

SIDI 1. One day, a woman came into the shop to buy some bread. She paid with several coins, one of which was false, and completely worthless.

The baker gives the woman back her coin. The woman returns it.

The baker stood firm, and told the woman that the piece of money was so obviously fake, that even his dog could pick it out.

BAKER. . . . Chance, Chance!

SIDI 1. Immediately I leaped onto the counter. The baker threw the money down in front of me.

BAKER. Look at these coins, Chance. Tell me which one is false.

*Sidi 2 examines and sniffs each coin and then sets his paw
on the bad one, separates it from the rest, and stares his
master in the face, to await approval.*

SIDI 1. The baker was staggered. He had only called me over
to make fun of the woman and never thought for a moment
that I would do as he asked. The woman changed the bad
coin for a good one and left, stunned into silence. As soon
as she left, my master called in some neighbours and told
them what had happened, boasting about his miraculous dog
with the magic gift of telling good money from bad.

People came from far and wide to see me and every time
they did, they bought a loaf of bread. Before long, my
master had more business than he could manage and he told
his neighbours I was worth my weight in gold.

Soon after this, a woman with a friendly face came to buy
some bread.

*The 2nd Customer throws down six coins on the counter.
Sidi 2 places his paw on one of the coins and looks up at
the woman.*

2ND CUSTOMER. Yes, you are quite right: that is the bad one

*The woman beckons for Sidi 2 to come with her. He
hesitates for a moment and then follows her out of the shop.*

Several streets away, she stopped at a house and beckoned
me in saying,

2ND CUSTOMER. You won't regret following me

He follows her in.

SIDI 1. When I went in I saw a beautiful young lady doing
embroidery. This lady, who had a smile as soft as hope, was
the friendly woman's daughter. She was also a good
sorceress, as I found out later.

2ND CUSTOMER. Daughter. I have brought you the famous
baker's dog, who can tell good money from bad. Remember
when I first heard about him, I had a hunch he was a man
changed into a dog. Today, I went to buy some bread from
that baker, and witnessed for myself the miracles this dog

can do. Now tell me, daughter, am I mistaken in my suspicion?

SORCERESS. No, mother, you are not. As I shall prove.

Sorceress dips her hand into a basin of water and throws it into Sidi 2's face with the words:

If you were cursed by evil plan
By the power of water change back to a man !

Sidi 2 returns to his old self.

SIDI 2. My debt to you is greater than I could ever repay.

SIDI 1. After I had told her who I was, I gave an account of my marriage to Amina, her curious eating, the horrible sight I saw in the graveyard and how I came to be changed into a dog.

SORCERESS. Sidi Nu'uman, let us hear no more talk of debts. It is enough for me to have helped such an honest man as you. I know Amina of old I am not at all surprised to learn of her wickedness. She must be punished once and for all. Wait here a moment.

She goes into a closet.

2ND CUSTOMER. My daughter knows as much magic as Amina, but she makes good use of it.

Sorceress returns.

SORCERESS. Take this bottle, go home immediately, and hide in your bedroom. As soon as Amina comes in, run down into the yard, and meet her face to face. At that moment, when she turns her back to run away, have the bottle ready and throw this potion at her, pronouncing clearly and boldly:

By the power of potion brewed over time
Receive the punishment for your crime!

SIDI 2. By the power of potion brewed over time

SIDI 2 AND SORCERESS.
    Receive the punishment for your crime

SORCERESS. I will tell you no more. You shall see the result.

Sorceress and second customer disappear.

Sidi 2 waits in his bedroom. Amina enters and meets her face to face: she screams and turns about to run to the door. He throws the potion over her She freezes.

SIDI 2.
By the power of potion brewed over time
Receive the punishment for your crime!

. *Amina transforms into a horse. Sidi 2 grabs her by the mane. He then rides her in a repeat of the first time we meet Sidi 1.Eventually, they leave the space.*

Sidi 2 echoes first entrance of Sidi 1, riding and beating a horse.

SIDI 1. And I have ridden her and beaten her the same way every day, ever since. I hope your majesty will now understand my strange conduct yesterday. Perhaps you will agree that I have shown such a cruel and wicked woman more patience than she deserves.

HAROUN. Your story is quite remarkable, and the wickedness of your wife inexcusable. Therefore I can forgive some of your harshness towards her. However, being turned into an animal is surely punishment enough and you should not seek to hurt her any more. Thirst for revenge is like a deadly, climbing weed. If it lays its roots in your thoughts, it will not stop till it has strangled your heart and poisoned your soul. To be free, you must forgive.

SHAHRAZAD. The wise Caliphsignified by the bowing of his head that Sidi Nu'uman was free to go. Sidi Nu'uman, kissed the ground before him and retired.

Sidi strokes his horse and leads it away.

Promise

The King's room.Dawn.

Sound of a sword being sharpened.

Enter Vizier. He is now an old, old man. He has just entered when the King signals for him to go. Without stopping he turns round and exits.

SHAHRAZAD. The day melted into night.

DINARZAD. And an hour before dawn

SHAHRAYAR. King Shahrayar said:

What story do you have for me tonight?

SHAHRAZAD. A trifling tale, my lord.

SHAHRAYAR. One of many hundreds of trifling tales you have told me already.

SHAHRAZAD. Eight hundred and seventeen, my lord.

SHAHRAYAR. Your wily woman's tongue has saved your pretty head eight hundred and seventeen times. That's a long time.

SHAHRAZAD. Two years, two months, three weeks and four days.

SHAHRAYAR. I can't seem to resist your stories my crafty queen. Your trick is working. Well go on. Begin.

Shahrazad doesn't speak.

SHAHRAZAD. Speak.

Shahrazad remains silent.

SHAHRAYAR. I'm listening.

She is still silent.

I command you to tell me your story.

Shahrazad whispers to Dinarzad.

SHAHRAYAR. Well what is she saying?

DINARZAD. She says she dare not speak. In case she tries to trick you with her cunning woman's words.

SHAHRAYAR. Tell her, I want to hear her story.

Dinarzad whispers to Shahrazad. Shahrazad whispers back..

DINARZAD. She says are you sure?

SHAHRAYAR. Tell her Yes!

Dinarzad whispers to her again. Shahrazad. whispers back.

DINARZAD. Really sure?

SHAHRAYAR. Yes. And stop whispering!!!

DINARZAD. The queen would like permission to ask a question, my lord.

SHAHRAYAR. Go on then.

Dinarzad whispers to her.

SHAHRAYAR. ONE MORE WHISPER AND I'LL HAVE BOTH YOUR HEADS OFF!

SHAHRAZAD. Your majesty.

SHAHRAYAR. Wife.

SHAHRAZAD. What would you do if the well of my stories runs dry?

SHAHRAYAR. I would no longer have an excuse to save you from death.

SHAHRAZAD. But what would you do? After that?

SHAHRAYAR. I would manage perfectly well.

SHAHRAZAD. I'm relieved, my lord.

SHAHRAYAR. But that will never happen. Will it?

SHAHRAZAD. As there are so many grains of sand in the desert, there are only so many stories in my head. They are sure to run out one day. And on that day, I must die. For you have given your word.

SHAHRAYAR. I have.

SHAHRAZAD. And a King's word is as precious as water.

SHAHRAYAR. It is.

SHAHRAZAD. Shall I start then?

SHAHRAYAR. What?

SHAHRAZAD. My Story.

SHAHRAYAR. Of course.

SHAHRAZAD. Very well.

Listen . . .

The Story of the Envious Sisters

SHAHRAZAD. There was once a King in Persia called Khusrau Shah.

One evening he went walking in the poorest area of the city, with his loyal vizier, when he overheard laughter coming from the humblest house in the street. He approached, and peeking through a crack in the door, he saw three sisters sitting on a sofa having an after dinner chat. They were talking about wishes.

ELDEST SISTER. I wish I could marry the King's Baker. For then I would eat my belly full of bread. And royal bread is the finest in the city, said the eldest.

SECOND SISTER. I wish I could marry the King's cook. For then I would eat the most excellent meats. And meats are much tastier than bread, added the second sister.

YOUNGEST. Then the youngest sister . . .

ELDEST. . . . who was very beautiful . . .

SECOND. . . . and more charming and modest than the others said:

YOUNGEST. I wish I could marry the King. For I would give him a beautiful baby prince, with hair like threads of silver and gold. When he cries his tears will be pearls and when he smiles his crimson lips will be fresh rose buds.

KING. The next day at the Palace, the King ordered his Vizier to bring the three sisters before him.

They kiss the floor before him. They stand.

Last night you each made a wish. You wished to be married to my baker. Your wish shall be granted today. You wished to marry my cook. Your wish shall be granted today. And you wished to marry me. Your wish shall be granted today..

Youngest sister throws herself on floor.

Forgive me, your majesty, but my wish was only made by way of fun. I am not worthy of this honour.

The two elder sisters see her doing this and reluctantly copy.

ELDEST SISTERS. Forgive us, your majesty . . . ..

KING (*interrupting*). Silence! It shall be so. Everyone's wish shall be fulfilled.

THREE SISTERS. The weddings were celebrated that day . . .

TWO ELDEST. . . . but in very different style.

ELDEST. The eldest sister's marriage was celebrated in the pantry surrounded by sacks of flour.

SECOND. The second sister's marriage was celebrated in the kitchen surrounded by pots and pans.

YOUNGEST. And the youngest sister was celebrated in the Royal Garden surrounded by jasmine and almond blossom.

ELDEST. Although their wishes had been granted . . .

SECOND. . . . the two elder sisters thought the difference between their weddings . . .

TWO ELDEST. . . . grossly unfair.

ELDEST. Their hearts were seized by a snake-like envy . . .

SECOND. . . . which not only strangled their own joy . . .

YOUNGEST. . . . but pierced their younger sister's happiness like a spiteful fang.

ELDEST. Well sister, what do you think of our grand little sister? Isn't she a fine one to be queen?

SECOND. I must say, I have no idea what the King sees in her. To be so bewitched by the little madam. You are much more deserving. In fairness he should have chosen you.

ELDEST. Sister I wouldn't have batted an eyelid if the King had picked you, but that he should prefer that pert slut makes my blood boil. However I will be revenged. And you I think are of the same mind.

SECOND. Let us put our heads together and see if we can come up with a plan to bring her, swiftly, to a nasty end.

ELDEST. From then on, whenever they visited the queen, their sister . . .

SECOND. . . . they would keep their vipers tongues hidden behind painted smiles . . .

YOUNGEST. . . . and she would welcome them warmly and simply and treat them with the same love she always had.

Some months after their marriage, the queen found she was expecting a baby. The good news spread throughout Persia.

ELDEST. The sisters came to give their best wishes . . .

SECOND. . . . and offered to be by their sister's side when the baby was born . . .

TWO ELDEST. . . . as her midwives.

The actor playing Bahman makes the sound of a baby crying.

YOUNGEST. The queen gave birth to a young prince as bright as morning.

ELDEST. But neither his sweetness . . .

SECOND. . . . nor his beauty . . .

TWO ELDEST. . . . could melt the icy hearts of the ruthless sisters.

ELDEST. They wrapped him in a coarse blanket, dropped him into a basket and floated him down a stream which ran past the queen's apartment.

SECOND. They then declared:

TWO ELDEST. She gave birth to a dead dog.

They produce the dead dog.

KING. When the King was told, the world turned dark before his eyes and he ordered the queen's head to be cut off.

VIZIER. But the kind Vizier stopped him, pleading that the queen could not be blamed for something that was not of her doing but nature's.

BAHMAN. Meanwhile, the basket, in which the little baby lay floated downstream past the palace and through the King's gardens.

STEWARD. By chance the Steward of the King's Garden was waking past. When he saw the basket bobbing by, he fished it out and peered in. He was astonished to see a tiny baby sleeping inside.

The Steward took the baby to his house and showed him to his wife.

WIFE. The wife received the child with great joy, and took pleasure in looking after him as if he was her own.

YOUNGEST. A year later, the queen had another baby prince.

The actor playing Perviz makes the sound of a baby crying.

TWO ELDEST. The wicked sisters were no kinder to him than the first.

FIRST. They put him in a basket and floated him down the stream . . .

SECOND. . . . . announcing . . .

TWO ELDEST. She gave birth to a cat.

They show the dead cat.

KING. This time the King was determined to cut off the young queen's head . . .

VIZIER. . . . but again the vizier stopped him pleading:

Let her live.

STEWARD. By happy chance, the Steward went walking by the stream again that day. So he took the second child to his wife and asked her to take as good care of it as the first.

WIFE. This suited her as well as it did her husband.

QUEEN. The third time the queen became pregnant, she gave birth to a princess.

The actor playing Parizade makes the sound of a baby crying.

TWO ELDEST. The poor child suffered the same fate as her brothers.

SECOND. This time the sisters couldn't find an animal . . .

ELDEST. . . . so they took a piece of wood and showed it, saying:

TWO ELDEST. She gave birth to a mole.

KING. The King could no longer contain himself.

This woman wants to fill my palace with monsters? She is a monster herself and I will rid the world of her.

He pronounced a sentence of death and ordered the Grand Vizier to see it carried out.

VIZIER. Your majesty, laws are made to punish crimes. The three strange births of the queen were not her fault. She is to be pitied not punished. Remove her from your eyes and heart, which is punishment enough, but let her live

KING. Very well. But it shall be on one condition: That at least once a day, for the rest of her life, she curses the day she was born. Let a cell be built for her next to the mosque, with iron bars for windows and throw her in. Dress her in clothes that scratch her skin. And everyone that goes past shall spit in her face. See it done.

VIZIER. The Vizier knew better than to question the King in his rage. So he did as he was told . . .

ELDEST SISTERS. . . . to the great pleasure of the two envious sisters.

The Queen is thrown into a cell. Passers-by spit.

STEWARD That same day, the Steward was walking past the stream, and he took the third child to his wife and asked her to take as good care of it as the first two . . .

WIFE. . . . which she did most gladly.

TWO PRINCES. The two princes . . .

PRINCESS. . . . and the princess . . .

STEWARD. . . . were brought up by the Steward . . .

STEWARD'S WIFE. . . . and his wife . . .

STEWARD AND WIFE. . . . with all the tenderness of a true father and mother.

THREE CHILDREN. They were named after the kings and queens of Persia.

BAHMAN. They eldest prince was named Bahman. He was gentle and kind.

PERVIZ. The second was named Perviz. He was bold and headstrong.

PARIZADE. And the Princess was named Parizade.

BAHMAN. She was enchantingly beautiful . . .

PERVIZ. . . . and exceptionally clever.

STEWARD. As soon as the princes were old enough, the Steward provided them with the best teachers money could buy.

PARIZADE. Even though the princess was much younger, she would join in all their lessons and would often outshine them.

STEWARD The Steward was delighted with his adopted children. So he set about building them a grand country house. He decked the rooms with priceless paintings and splendid furniture. He filled the garden with blazing flowers and fragrant shrubs. Then he stocked the nearby land with deer, so that the princes and princess could go hunting.

He lived in the house with the two princes, Bahman and Perviz, and princess Parizade for six months, when one day he shut his eyes and died.

PERVIZ. His wife had died some years before and his death was so sudden that he never told them the secret of their birth.

PARIZADE. The princes and the princess wept bitter tears of grief for the loving man they thought their father.

ALL THREE. But they were comforted by their beautiful house and lived there together in harmony.

WOMAN. One day, when the two princes were out hunting, an old religious woman arrived at the house. When she had said her prayers, she sat down with Parizade and chatted with her.

PARIZADE. Eventually Parizade asked her what she thought of the house.

WOMAN. Madam, it would be the King of houses but for three things.

PARIZADE. And what three things are they? I will do what I can to secure them.

WOMAN. The first of these things is the Talking Bird. This will draw a thousand coloured birds around it. The second is the singing tree. This will play a haunting harmony. The third is the Golden Water. This will form an everlasting fountain.

PARIZADE. I've never heard of such curious, wonderful things. Would you kindly tell me where they are?

WOMAN. Towards India, on the road that lies before your house. Whoever you send must travel twenty days. On the twentieth, they must ask the first person they meet where the talking bird, singing tree and golden fountain are. They shall be told.

If you find these three things, child, they will lead you to the truth about yourself.

PARIZADE. What do you mean?

WOMAN. And a fine lady shall be freed.

PARIZADE. I don't understand.

WOMAN. The road that lies before your house

She goes. Parizade is so wrapped up in the Old Woman's words that she doesn't notice her leave. She looks around, and realising she is alone, tries to remember her instructions.

PARIZADE. Towards India, on the road that lies before your house. Twenty days along.

Princess Parizade felt, in the pit of her stomach, that she had to have these things.

BROTHERS. When her brothers returned, they found their sister with her head weighed down as if her thoughts were made of lead.

BAHMAN. Sister, are you unwell or has some misfortune befallen you?

PERVIZ. Do not hide the truth from us, sister, unless you wish to harm our friendship.

PARIZADE. So she told her brothers what the old woman had said.

BAHMAN. Tell me the place and the way there and I will leave tomorrow.

Early the next morning, Prince Bahman prepared his horse.

Parizade and Bahman embrace.

Bahman takes out a knife.

Here sister, take this knife and every now and then, look at the blade. If it is clean, it is a sign I am alive. If it is stained with blood, then you must believe me dead, and pray for me.

On the twentieth day of his journey, he saw, by the side of
the road a wise old man sitting under a tree.

Good day, good father. I have come a long way in search of
the talking bird, the singing tree and the golden water. I
know these things are nearby. Could you show me the way
to them?

OLD MAN. Friendship forbids me to tell you

BAHMAN. Why?

OLD MAN. A great number of fine gentlemen, as brave and
courageous as you, have passed by here and asked me the
very same question. When I tried my best to persuade them
to turn back, they wouldn't listen. At last, against my better
judgement, I have told them the way and not one of them
has ever come back. Son, if the gift of life means anything
to you, go home now.

BAHMAN. I have a knife. If anyone attacks me I shall use it.

OLD MAN. What if your enemies are invisible?.

BAHMAN. Good father, no matter what you say, you will
never persuade me to alter my course.

OLD MAN. Since I cannot persuade you to see sense, take this
ball. When you are on horseback, throw it and follow it to
the foot of a mountain where it will stop rolling. Leave your
horse and start climbing the slope. You will see a large
number of black stones and hear many threatening voices
pressing you to turn round. They will try everything they
can to stop you reaching the top of the mountain. But
remember, whatever you hear behind you, however cruel,
vicious or threatening: do not look back. For if you do, you
will be turned into black stone like the other gentlemen
before you. If you manage to escape this danger and reach
the top of the mountain you will see a cage. In that cage is
the bird you seek. Ask him for the singing tree and golden
water and he will show you. May the Heavens preserve you.

BAHMAN. Bahman thanked the wise old man, mounted his
horse and threw the ball before him.

The ball rolls away. When it reaches the foot of the mountain, it stops.

The company become stones.

He looked up the mountain and saw the black stones, but had not gone four steps when the voices started.

The voices start quietly and escalate with every step he takes till they reach a murderous and deafening cacophony. Each actor repeats / improvises around the lines below. The same format is used for each attempt.

1. You'll never make it to the top. A little weakling like you?

   Laughter etc.

2. Turn around. There's a wolf behind you.

3. That's it. Carry on. Just see what awaits you at the top of the slope! You are walking towards your death, etc.

4. Go home. Your family are ill. They need your help, etc.

5. You snivelling little wretch. You cockroach. You snake, etc.

6. I've got a surprise for you, sweet child, come and get your surprise.

7. It's the devil's trick. Turn back. This is the voice of your father. Turn back!

   Eventually Bahman's courage gives way and he turns. Instantly he is turned into stone.

PARIZADE. Just then, Princess Parizade pulled the knife out of its sheath, as she did many times a day, to see if her brother was safe. Her heart froze to stone in her chest when she saw that the point was dripping with blood.

She throws down the knife.

Oh my dear brother I have been the cause your death. I wish I had never met the old religious woman. Why did she tell me of the bird, the tree and the water?

PERVIZ. Our dear brother's death must not prevent us from pursuing our plan. Tomorrow I shall go myself.

PARIZADE. The princess begged him not to go . . .

PERVIZ. . . . but he was determined. Before he went, he left her a necklace of a hundred pearls, telling her, from time to time, to run her fingers along them.

If they move, I am alive. If they are fixed, then you know I am dead.

On the twentieth day of his journey, Prince Perviz met the wise old man. Prince Perviz asked him, the same way his brother had, where he could find the talking bird, singing tree and golden water . . .

OLD MAN. . . . and the Wise Old Man pleaded with Prince Perviz to go home as he had to Prince Bahman.

PERVIZ. Good father, I have thought too long and hard about this plan to give up now.

OLD MAN. As Prince Perviz could not be stopped, the Wise Old Man handed him a ball. Then he gave Prince Perviz the same warning he had given to Prince Bahman, about the black stones and the threatening voices.

But remember, whatever you hear behind you, however cruel, vicious or threatening: do not look back.

PERVIZ. Prince Perviz mounted his horse, took leave of the wise man with a low bow and threw the ball before him.

The ball rolls away. When it reaches the foot of the mountain, it stops.

Full company become stones, as before. Same escalation of voices, but louder.

Prince Perviz gets very near the bird when the other voices stop and a male stone just behind him speaks.

STONE. Stop there, foolish youth, my sword longs to punish your insolence

When he hears this, Perviz draws his sword and turns around. He is immediately turned into stone.

PARIZADE. Just then, Princess Parizade was pulling on the pearls of her necklace, as she did many times a day, when all of a sudden, they would not stir. She knew then for certain that Prince Perviz was dead.

The next morning, she set out on the same road as her brothers. On the twentieth day, she met the wise old man.

Parizade asked the old man where she could find the talking bird, singing tree and golden water . . .

OLD MAN. . . . and the Wise Old Man pleaded with her to turn round, as he had with her brothers.

PARIZADE. And give up my plan? I am sure I shall succeed.

OLD MAN. Because she would not heed his advice, the Wise Old Man gave her the ball and repeated the warning he had given to Prince Bahman and Prince Perviz about the dreadful danger of the black stones and the threatening voices.

PARIZADE. From what you say, the only danger I face is getting to the cage without hearing the threatening voices. But that can be overcome quite simply.

WISE MAN. How?

PARIZADE. By stopping my ears with cotton.

WISE MAN. Of all the people who have asked me the way, I do not know of anyone who thought of that. If you must go, by all means try your trick. But remember, if you should hear anything on the mountain, however cruel, vicious or threatening: do not look back.

PARIZADE. After thanking him, she rode away and threw the ball before her.

The ball rolls away. When it reaches the foot of the mountain it stops.

Full company become stones, as before. Same escalation of volume, but even louder. She gets close to the bird who is a tiny glove puppet in a cage, operated by the Queen.

BIRD. Brave lady, if I have to be a slave I would rather be your slave than any in the world, since you have won me so courageously. From this moment, I swear a lifelong loyalty to you and promise to fulfil your every need.

PARIZADE. Thank you bird.

BIRD. I know who you really are and I can tell you. You are not who think you are.

PARIZADE. What do you mean?

BIRD. You will find out in Allah's good time.

PARIZADE. Bird, I have been told that there is a singing tree nearby. I want to know where it is.

BIRD. Turn around. You will see a wood behind you. You will find the tree there.

She picks up the bird.

PARIZADE. The princess went into the wood. Her ears soon led her to the tree.

Company become singing tree.

BIRD. Break off a branch and plant it in your garden. In a short time it will grow into as fine a tree as you see here.

PARIZADE. Bird, I also want to find the golden water. Can you show me to it?

The bird showed her the place that was very nearby and she went and filled a silver flask she had brought.

Company become fountain.

PARIZADE. I have one more request. My brothers were turned into black stones. I want you to free them.

BIRD. Look around and you will see a pitcher of water.

PARIZADE. I see it.

BIRD. Pick it up, go down the hill and sprinkle some on every black stone. You shall soon find your brothers.

Parizade picks up the pitcher and goes down the hill sprinkling water on every black stone. As soon as she does, it immediately turns into a man or a horse.

PARIZADE. Before long she found her brothers.

They embrace

BAHMAN. She gave Prince Bahman the branch from the singing tree . . .

PERVIZ. . . . and Prince Perviz the golden water to carry . . .

ALL THREE. . . . and they set off for home.

PARIZADE. When the princess arrived, she placed the cage in the garden.

As soon as the bird starts to sing colourful birds swoop and glide around it.

BAHMAN. Then she planted the branch of the singing tree.

The tree sprouts up, each leaf singing a delightful tune and all joining together to play a harmonious concert.

PERVIZ. After that she poured the flask of golden water into a marble pool.

A fountain shoots up.

BAHMAN. Some days later, Prince Bahman . . .

PERVIZ. . . . and Prince Perviz . . .

TWO PRINCES. . . . went hunting in a nearby wood.

KING. As it happened, hunting in the same wood was the King . . .

PERVIZ. . . . and whilst going down a narrow lane, they chanced upon him.

They kiss the ground before the King..

BAHMAN. When the princes stood up, they seemed so at ease . . .

PERVIZ. . . . and yet so modest . . .

KING. . . . that the King's heart warmed to them. He asked who they were, and where they lived.

BAHMAN. Sir, we are the sons of the late Steward of the King's Garden and we live in a house nearby.

KING. Very good. I need somewhere to rest this evening. I should like to visit you.

PERVIZ. Your majesty, we would be honoured.

BAHMAN. Princes Bahman . . .

PERVIZ. . . . and Perviz pointed the King's courtiers to the house . . .

PARIZADE. . . . and hurried home to tell their sister.

We must prepare a banquet for his majesty. I shall ask the talking bird what food the King likes best.

She goes to the bird.

PARIZADE. Bird, The King will be coming to visit tonight. What shall we give him to eat.

BIRD. Let your cooks prepare a dish of cucumbers stuffed with pearls.

PARIZADE. Cucumbers stuffed with pearls? You're talking rubbish, bird. The King wants something good to eat, not new jewellery. Besides where would I get enough pearls for such a dish?

BIRD. Mistress, have faith. Go now to the foot of the singing tree, dig under it and you will find what you want.

Parizade digs and finds a precious gold box filled with pearls.

PARIZADE. Parizade called the head cook to her.

Tonight you must prepare the King's favourite speciality: cucumbers stuffed with pearls.

She opens the box.

2ND COOK. Cucumbers stuffed with pearls?

PARIZADE. I'm surprised at you, Cook. Surely you don't mean to say you've never heard of such a fine dish?

2ND COOK. Of course I have madam.

The cook takes the box and goes away.

Then, the princess told the servants to make ready for the visit of the King.

King's arrival. Parizade goes before him and kisses the floor.

BROTHERS. This is our sister.

The King helps her up.

KING. I hope to get to know you better, madam, after I have seen the house.

PARIZADE. So the princess showed him the golden water, singing tree, and the talking bird, who sat in his cage in the hall.

BIRD. The King is welcome here. Allah spare him and grant him a long life.

KING. Bird I thank you and am overjoyed to have found in you the King of birds..

The bird bows. They sit down to eat.

As soon as the King saw the dish of delicious juicy cucumbers set before him, he reached out and took one. But when he cut it, he was astonished to find it full of pearls.

Cucumbers stuffed with pearls? Pearls are not to be eaten! What's the meaning of this?

BIRD. Can your majesty be so amazed at seeing cucumbers stuffed with pearls? Yet you readily believe that the queen, your wife, gave birth to a dog, a cat and a piece of wood.

KING. I believed it because I was told by her midwives.

BIRD. Those midwives were the queen's wicked sisters, who out of envy and revenge lied to your majesty. Awake from your sleep of ignorance : The brothers and sister that you see before you are your own children. Found by the Steward

of your garden who brought them up and educated them as
his own.

KING. My heart whispered the truth from the moment I met
you.

They embrace.

And now the world shall embrace you as worthy children to
the royal house of Persia.

ALL THREE. So by torchlight, they set out for the city on
their horses.

KING. As soon as they reached the palace, the King ordered
the Chief Vizier to bring the queen's envious sisters
immediately to trial.

VIZIER. And after they were found guilty . . .

ELDEST SISTER. . . . they were each cut into four pieces . . .

SECOND SISTER. . . . and fed to the dogs.

KING. In the meantime the King Khusrau Shah . . .

ALL THREE. . . . followed by his three children . . .

BIRD. . . . and the talking bird . . .

ALL FOUR. . . . went to the great mosque.

The First Sister is freed from her cell..

KING. I come to plead for your pardon for the wrong I have
done you, and to make amends. Here is your crown, and
here are two angelic princes . . .

They bow before her.

. . . and a heavenly princess –

She bows.

Our children.

They embrace

QUEEN. Warm light flooded the queen's heart when she saw
her sacred children, after the darkness she had suffered for
so many years.

SHAHRAZAD. The news spread throughout the town, and crowds of people came to meet the family as they returned to the palace. The people's eyes smiled not only on the queen, the princes and the princess, but on the talking bird who, by his sweet song, had drawn fluttering flocks of other birds around him. They followed him, swooping from tree to tree, gliding from one roof to another. And nothing was seen but thousands of candles or heard but cries of joy from the golden domes of the palace to the poorest edge of town.

The Story without an Ending

Dawn. The Palace.

SHAHRAZAD. My lord, this story shows the pain that follows, when a King acts without thinking and shuts his ears to the truth.

SHAHRAYAR. Shahrazad, even a King can lose his way. But he can find it again when the door to his heart is opened.

Pause.

DINARZAD. What story will you have for us tonight, sister?

Enter Vizier.

VIZIER. The executioner awaits your command, my lord.

SHAHRAZAD. Tonight I had planned to tell a special story. About another King who loses his way. It is called The Story Without an Ending. But I can't seem to remember it. The well of my stories has run dry. I fear I must go to the headsman.

SHAHRAYAR. The Executioner cannot act without royal decree.

SHAHRAZAD. But haven't you sworn that if the well of my stories dries up, I must die?

Silence.

Vizier, didn't you hear the King say this?

VIZIER. Well . . .

SHAHRAZAD. Didn't you?

VIZIER. I did.

SHAHRAZAD. Sister, you heard this didn't you?

DINARZAD. Yes.

SHAHRAZAD. Unless the King has broken his word, I must go to the executioner.

SHAHRAYAR. Curses on your impudence. Go then, imbecile. GET OUT! Vizier see it done!

VIZIER. Yes, my lord.

They exit. Shahrayar is alone. As he searches for things to do, he becomes lonely and scared. Characters from the stories visit the room. They move around him, speaking fragments of lines form their stories. He tries to block them out. The little beggar stumbles past.

VIZIER FROM ENVIOUS. Laws are made to punish crimes.

Two of the dogs from 'The Wife who Wouldn't Eat' run past.

ALI BABA. OPEN SESAME!

TALKING BIRD. I know who you really are. And I can tell you. It is not who you think you are.

Marjana dances by.

ES-SINDIBAD. Till that moment I believed I would never leave the valley alive, but now I started to see a way out.

The rukh swirls around him. The room is full of characters from Shahrazad's stories.

KING. Shahrazad! Shahrazad! Come back here! Vizier, Headsman, Stop! Stop! STOOOOP!

The characters exit.

Shahrazad, Dinarzad, Vizier and court enter.

SHAHRAZAD. You called, your majesty.

SHAHRAYAR. Wife, if you insist on following this ridiculous course, I shall not stand in your way.

SHAHRAZAD. Thank you, your majesty.

SHAHRAYAR. But before you go, I have one last request.

SHAHRAZAD. Certainly. How may I be of help?

SHAHRAYAR. Try to remember your story. The Story Without an Ending.

SHAHRAZAD. I can't.

SHAHRAYAR. Please wife. One last story.

SHAHRAZAD. I'll see what I can do. (*She thinks hard.*) Very Well, now. Listen . . .

Once there was a strong, brave King who loved to laugh. One day, he was betrayed by his wicked wife and lost all his love of women and his happiness. A lonely black night fell in his heart and his soul was possessed by a dark demon.

There is not a single good woman anywhere on the face of the earth, he would say.

Although he looked the same on the outside, on the inside, the good King of old was replaced by a cruel, merciless tyrant. Every night he would marry a different woman and the next morning, he would have her killed. This way no one could ever cheat on him again, and he was safe. Darkness spread from his heart around the palace and hung heavy over the city. Many young women died. The people feared for their daughters and grew angry and confused.

Where has our big hearted King disappeared to? they asked.

Now the King's Vizier had two daughters and the eldest daughter was blessed with a magic power. Fate had decreed that she use this magic power to slay the dark demon in the King's soul and bring the daylight back to his world. When she saw him, she knew that she was also fated to love him, with a love as true as the sky and as mysterious as the moon. This woman was called Shahrazad and her magic was the magic of stories.

Night after moonlit night, she would pour the magic medicine of her stories into his ears. And little by little, dawn started to break in his heart, and a tiny flower laid its precious roots there. Before long, the daughters of the city walked freely in the sunshine. And news that the King no longer lived in darkness travelled across the land like a white horse of hope and over the sparkling sea, bathing those that heard it in warm light.

After a long, long time, the Queen found that she was expecting the King's baby. When she had told him her stories for 1001 nights, she tested the King to see if the flower in his heart had bloomed and whether he was ready to save the life of his wife and unborn child.

There the story runs out, my lord. Perhaps you know the ending . . .

Shahrayar falls to his knees and cries.

SHAHRAYAR. Shahrazad, forgive me.

SHAHRAZAD. It is not me but your people you must ask to forgive you. I forgave you long ago.

SHAHRAYAR. There is a good woman on the face of this earth.

SHAHRAZAD (*to Dinarzad*). There are many.

SHAHRAYAR. Vizier.

VIZIER. Yes, my lord.

SHAHRAYAR. Publish in the city that King Shahrayar has lifted the death sentence on Queen Shahrazad.

VIZIER. Certainly, my lord.

SHAHRAYAR. And that she is expecting the King's baby.

VIZIER. Yes, my lord.

SHAHRAYAR. Oh and Vizier.

VIZIER. Yes, my lord.

SHAHRAYAR. Have the day off.

VIZIER. Yes, my lord.

SHAHRAYAR. Now let us celebrate the freedom of our gracious queen.

SHAHRAZAD. And the welcome return of the good King.

She offers her hand.

They kiss.

Dance. A celebration of rebirth.

After dance, full company join for the Epilogue.

Epilogue

ACTOR 1. Celebrations spread throughout the land.

ACTOR 2. With eating and drinking and dancing for many days.

ACTOR 3. Afterwards, in honour of the young women who had lost their lives, the King called together his scribes and scholars

ACTOR 4. and, ordered them to write down every one of Shahrazad's enchanting stories into a book.

ACTOR 5. One story for each of the young women,

ACTOR. 6. And one story for each night that the King's heart lived in darkness.

SHAHRAYAR. And the book lived longer than the King . . .

SHAHRAZAD. . . . and Shahrazad . . .

DINARZAD. . . . and their children . . .

ACTOR 1. . . . and their children's children . . .

ACTOR 2. . . . even the city itself . . .

ACTOR 3. . . . and they called this Book Alf Layla wa Layla . . .

ACTOR. 4. . . . 1001 Nights . . .

ACTOR 5. . . . but even now, when the desert sky is as dark as doom . . .

ACTOR. 6. . . . and the sand glows silver in the moonlight . . .

SHAHRAYAR. . . . on the site where the old city used to be . . .

DINARZAD. . . . you can hear the sweet voice of a beautiful young woman, weaving magical tales into the night.

SHAHRAZAD. Listen . . .

Lights out.

The End.

A Nick Hern Book

Arabian Nights first published in Great Britain in 1998
as a paperback original by Nick Hern Books Limited,
14 Larden Road, London W3 7ST in association with
the Young Vic Theatre, The Cut, London SE1 8LZ

Typeset by Country Setting, Kingsdown, Kent CT14 8ES
Printed and bound in Great Britain by Cox and Wyman Ltd,
Reading, Berks

ISBN 1 85459 432 X

A CIP catalogue record for this book is available from
the British Library